Lecture Notes in Computer Science   11091

Commenced Publication in 1973
Founding and Former Series Editors:
Gerhard Goos, Juris Hartmanis, and Jan van Leeuwen

Editorial Board

More information about this series at http://www.springer.com/series/7410

Sokratis K. Katsikas · Cristina Alcaraz (Eds.)

Security
and Trust Management

14th International Workshop, STM 2018
Barcelona, Spain, September 6–7, 2018
Proceedings

 Springer

Editors
Sokratis K. Katsikas 🔟
Open University of Cyprus
Latsia
Cyprus

Cristina Alcaraz 🔟
University of Malaga
Malaga
Spain

and

Norwegian University of Science
 and Technology
Gjøvik
Norway

ISSN 0302-9743   ISSN 1611-3349 (electronic)
Lecture Notes in Computer Science
ISBN 978-3-030-01140-6   ISBN 978-3-030-01141-3 (eBook)
https://doi.org/10.1007/978-3-030-01141-3

Library of Congress Control Number: 2018955425

LNCS Sublibrary: SL4 – Security and Cryptology

This Springer imprint is published by the registered company Springer Nature Switzerland AG
The registered company address is: Gewerbestrasse 11, 6330 Cham, Switzerland

Preface

This volume contains the papers presented at the 14th International Workshop on Security and Trust Management (STM 2018). The workshop was co-located with the 23rd European Symposium on Research in Computer Security (ESORICS 2018) and was held in Barcelona, Spain, during September 6–7, 2018.

STM (Security and Trust Management) is a working group of ERCIM (European Research Consortium in Informatics and Mathematics). The STM workshop seeks submissions from academia, industry, and government that present novel research on all theoretical and practical aspects of security and trust in ICTs.

STM 2018 attracted 28 high-quality submissions, each of which was assigned to three referees for review; the review process resulted in eight full papers being accepted to be presented and included in the proceedings. These contributions cover topics related to cryptosystems and applied cryptography; modelling and risk assessment; and trust computing.

We would like to express our deepest thanks to all those who assisted us in organizing the event and putting together the program. We are very grateful to the ERCIM STM Steering Committee, and particularly its chair, Pierangela Samarati, for entrusting us with organizing the workshop; to Nicholas Kolokotronis, for taking care of publicity; to Joaquin Garcia-Alfaro (ESORICS 2018 Workshops Chair) and Miquel Soriano (ESORICS 2018 General Chair) for their support in organizing the workshop and taking care of the logistics. Special thanks go to the members of the Program Committee for their timely and rigorous reviews that helped us greatly in putting together a stimulating program. Last, but by no means least, we would like to thank all the authors who submitted their work to the workshop and contributed to an interesting set of proceedings.

August 2018

Sokratis K. Katsikas
Cristina Alcaraz

Organization

Sokratis Katsikas (Chair)   Open University of Cyprus, Cyprus and Norwegian
                               University of Science and Technology, Norway
Cristina Alcaraz (Chair)   University of Malaga, Spain
Ken Barker   University of Calgary, Canada
David Chadwick   University of Kent, UK
Jorge Cuellar   Siemens AG, Corporate Technology, Germany
Sabrina De Capitani di   University of Milan, Italy
    Vimercati
Josep Domingo-Ferrer   Universitat Rovira i Virgili, Spain
Carmen Fernández-Gago   University of Malaga, Spain
Sara Foresti   University of Milan, Italy
Joaquin Garcia-Alfaro   Telecom SudParis, France
Vasileios Gkioulos   Norwegian University of Science and Technology,
                               Norway
Ehud Gudes   Ben-Gurion University, Israel
Nicholas Kolokotronis   University of the Peloponnese, Greece
Costas Lambrinoudakis   University of Piraeus, Greece
Giovanni Livraga   University of Milan, Italy
Fabio Martinelli   IIT-CNR, Italy
Sjouke Mauw   University of Luxembourg, Luxembourg
Catherine Meadows   Naval Research Laboratory, USA
Chris Mitchell   Royal Holloway, University of London, UK
Charles Morisset   Newcastle University, UK
Pankaj Pandey   Norwegian University of Science and Technology,
                               Norway
Günther Pernul   Universität Regensburg, Germany
Marinella Petrocchi   IIT-CNR, Italy
Benoit Poletti   Ministry of Economy/INCERT GIE, Luxembourg
Silvio Ranise   FBK-Irst, Italy
Pierangela Samarati   University of Milan, Italy
Ralf Sasse   ETH Zurich, Switzerland
Daniele Sgandurra   Royal Holloway, University of London, UK
Georgios Spathoulas   University of Thessaly, Greece
Fabian Van Den Broek   Open University in the Netherlands, The Netherlands

Contents

Cryptosystems and Applied Cryptography

Achieving Strong Security and Verifier-Local Revocation for Dynamic Group Signatures from Lattice Assumptions

Maharage Nisansala Sevwandi Perera[1(✉)] and Takeshi Koshiba[2]

[1] Graduate School of Science and Engineering,
Saitama University, Saitama, Japan
perera.m.n.s.119@ms.saitama-u.ac.jp
[2] Faculty of Education and Integrated Arts and Sciences,
Waseda University, Tokyo, Japan
tkoshiba@waseda.jp

Abstract. Both member registration and member revocation are essential features in group signature schemes. In ASIACRYPT 2016 Libert, Ling, Mouhartem, Nguyen, and Wang suggested a simple joining mechanism with their lattice-based group signature scheme with member registration. However, their scheme does not support member revocation. Verifier-local revocation is a member revocation approach in group signature schemes, which only requires the verifiers to keep the revocation messages while existing members have no burden. Since there is no workload for existing members related to revocation messages, verifier-local revocation method became the most suitable revocation approach for any environment. However, original group signature schemes with verifier-local revocability satisfy weaker security. This paper adds verifier-local revocation mechanism to the Libert's (ASIACRYPT 2016) scheme to produce a fully dynamic lattice-based group signature scheme with member registration and member revocation using verifier-local revocation mechanism. Moreover, the resulted scheme achieves stronger security than the security in the original group signature schemes with verifier-local revocation.

Keywords: Lattice-based group signatures · Verifier-local revocation
Almost-full anonymity · Dynamical-almost-full anonymity
Member registration

1 Introduction

Group Signature schemes introduced by Chaum and van Heyst [14] enable group members to sign messages on behalf of the group while hiding their identity (anonymity). However, in case of dispute, the tracing authority can cancel the anonymity of signatures to identify the signer (traceability). These two features,

© Springer Nature Switzerland AG 2018
S. K. Katsikas and C. Alcaraz (Eds.): STM 2018, LNCS 11091, pp. 3–19, 2018.
https://doi.org/10.1007/978-3-030-01141-3_1

anonymity and traceability allow group signatures to find applications in real-life. For instance, e-commerce systems, road-to-vehicle communication systems, and key-card access. In a theoretical manner, forming a secure and efficient group signature scheme that facilitates both member registration and revocation is both interesting and challenging task. Bellare et al. [4] (BMW03 model) proposed two formal and strong security notions called *full-anonymity* and *full-traceability* for static group signatures. Then Bellare et al. [5] used the BMW03 model to present a dynamic group signature scheme which supports only member registration. Recently, Bootle et al. [8] provided a security definition for fully dynamic group signatures.

In recent years, lattice-based group signatures have been an active research topic because lattice-based cryptography provides provable security under worst-case hardness assumptions. Gorden et al. [16] proposed the first lattice-based group signature scheme in 2010. However, the first lattice-based group signature scheme that supports member revocation was suggested by Langlois et al. [19]. The scheme in [19] manages member revocation using Verifier-local revocation (VLR) mechanism. On the other hand, the scheme presented by Libert et al. [20] provides member registration. The scheme in [20] provides a simple joining mechanism with zero-knowledge argument system that allows the valid signers to proof that their secret key is certified by the group manager. However, the scheme in [20] does not support member revocation. Thus the scheme in [20] is not fully dynamic. Ling et al. [22] presented a fully dynamic group signature scheme based on lattices using accumulators. Verifier-local revocation (VLR) mechanism is efficient than using accumulators. Especially, when considering large groups, VLR is more suitable than accumulators.

We focus on applying membership revocation facility using VLR to the scheme given in [20]. There are several revocation approaches. The simplest revocation method is that the group manager generates the group public key and secret keys of all members newly except for the revoked member and re-distributes the keys [3]. However, this is not suitable for large groups. Another approach is broadcasting a small public membership message to all signers and verifiers, as in [6,12]. However, still, signers have to obtain revocation details at the time of signing. On the other hand, Verifier-local Revocation (VLR) sends revocation messages only to the verifiers. Since the number of verifiers is less than the number of signers, VLR method seems to be the most suitable approach for any size of groups.

Verifier-Local Revocation (VLR) was proposed by Brickell [10] and formalized by Boneh et al. [7] in their group signature scheme. The *Verifier-local Revocation* (VLR) group signature scheme uses a token system, and when a member is revoked, the revoking member's token is added to a list called *Revocation List* (RL). Thus the verifier uses RL to authenticate the signer at the signature verification stage. In such manner, in VLR group signature schemes, the verifiers do "signature-check" and "revocation-check". Since VLR does not require to generate keys newly or keep track of revocation information with the existing members, it is more convenient than any other approach. When a member is revoked, VLR only asks to send the revocation information to the verifiers. Thus, VLR is suitable for any size of groups.

When applying VLR to an existing scheme, we have to focus on several problems. Since the original VLR group signature scheme based on lattices [19] relied on a weaker security notion called *selfless-anonymity*, when VLR is suggesting to an existing scheme, the existing scheme's security becomes weaker. Thus, if we want to make the resulting scheme's security stronger, then we have to consider a security notion like *almost-full anonymity* [25], which is for partially dynamic VLR schemes or *dynamical-almost-full anonymity* [24], which is for fully dynamic VLR schemes. Moreover, in general VLR schemes, revocation tokens are generated as a part of the secret signing key. But, when we apply the almost-full anonymity or the dynamical-almost-full anonymity, we have to separate generation of member revocation token from the secret signing key. Thus, we have to concern about the member revocation token generation without affecting the construction of the existing scheme.

This paper aims to achieve fully dynamic group signature scheme with strong security by proposing VLR technique to an existing member registration scheme with ease.

1.1   Our Contribution

This paper proposes a scheme by applying VLR revocation mechanism to the scheme given in [20]. The group signature scheme with VLR [19] uses revocation token, which is a part of the secret signing key. However, in case of the full-anonymity game, which is described in the BMW03 model, the adversary is given all the members secret signing keys. Hence, for the group signatures with VLR, achieving full-anonymity is technically difficult since we cannot give both the secret signing keys and the revocation tokens to the adversary at the anonymity game. If the revocation tokens are given to the adversary, he can execute the verification algorithm Verify with the revocation tokens of the challenged indices and identify the index which is used to generate the challenging signature. The scheme in [25] suggested a new security notion called almost-full anonymity, which does not provide any revocation tokens unless requested by the adversary and which does not generate the challenging signature for the indices whose revocation tokens are queried. The scheme in [24] presented a security notion called dynamical-almost-full anonymity, which is an extended version of the almost-full anonymity for fully dynamic group signature schemes. Moreover, if the secret signing keys are given to the adversary, then he can generate the revocation tokens of the challenged indices using the secret signing keys and execute Verify to identify the index, which is used to create the challenging signature. Thus, we use dynamical-almost-full anonymity to secure our scheme, and we use a vector related to the secret signing key (but not the part of the secret signing key) as the revocation token. However, since the group manager should know the revocation token, we select a vector which is generated by the group manager. Otherwise, a cheating member can present a fake revocation token to the group manager at the time of revoking or to the verifier at the time of signing.

This paper highlights the difficulties of achieving strong security while providing member revocation with VLR. Moreover, this paper shows how to accomplish strong security and member revocation with VLR without affecting the structure of the existing scheme in [20].

2   Preliminaries

2.1   Notations

For any integer $k \geq 1$, we denote the set of integers $\{1, \ldots, k\}$ by $[k]$. We denote matrices by bold upper-case letters such as $\mathbf{A}$, and vectors by bold lower-case letters, such as $\mathbf{x}$. We assume that all vectors are in column form. The concatenation of matrices $\mathbf{A} \in \mathbb{R}^{n \times m}$ and $\mathbf{B} \in \mathbb{R}^{n \times k}$ denoted by $[\mathbf{A}|\mathbf{B}] \in \mathbb{R}^{n \times (m+k)}$. The concatenation of vectors $\mathbf{x} \in \mathbb{R}^m$ and $\mathbf{y} \in \mathbb{R}^k$ denoted by $(\mathbf{x}\|\mathbf{y}) \in \mathbb{R}^{m+k}$. The Euclidean norm of $\mathbf{x}$ is denoted by $\|\mathbf{x}\|$ and the infinity norm is denoted by $\|\mathbf{x}\|_\infty$. The Euclidean norm of matrix $\mathbf{B} \in \mathbb{R}^{m \times n}$ with columns $(\mathbf{b}_i)_{i \leq n}$ is denoted by $\|\mathbf{B}\| = \max_{i \leq n} \|\mathbf{b}_i\|$. If $\mathbf{B}$ is a full column-rank, then its Gram-Schmidt marginalization is denoted by $\tilde{\mathbf{B}}$. If S is a finite set, the uniform distribution over S is denoted by $U(S)$. The action of sampling x according to the uniform distribution is denoted by $x \hookleftarrow U(S)$.

Throughout this paper, we present the security parameter as $\lambda > 0$ and the maximum number of members in a group as $N = 2^\ell \in \mathsf{poly}(\lambda)$. Then choose lattice parameter $n = \mathcal{O}(\lambda)$, prime modulus $q = \tilde{\mathcal{O}}(\ell n^3)$, dimension $m = 2n\lceil \log q \rceil$, Gaussian parameter $\sigma = \Omega(\sqrt{n \log q} \log n)$, infinity norm bounds $\beta = \sigma\omega(\log m)$ and $b = \sqrt{n}\omega(\log n)$. Choose a hash function $\mathcal{H} : \{0,1\}^* \to \{1,2,3\}^t$ for some $t = \omega(\log n)$, which will be modeled as a random oracle in the proof of security. Let χ be a b-bounded distribution over $\mathbb{Z}$.

2.2   Lattices

Let q be a prime and $\mathbf{B} = [\mathbf{b}_1|\cdots|\mathbf{b}_m] \in \mathbb{Z}_q^{r \times m}$ be linearly independent vectors in $\mathbb{Z}_q^r$. The r-dimensional lattice $\Lambda(\mathbf{B})$ for $\mathbf{B}$ is defined as

$$\Lambda(\mathbf{B}) = \{\mathbf{y} \in \mathbb{Z}^r \mid \mathbf{y} \equiv \mathbf{Bx} \bmod q \text{ for some } \mathbf{x} \in \mathbb{Z}_q^m\},$$

which is the set of all linear combinations of columns of $\mathbf{B}$. The value m is the rank of $\mathbf{B}$.

We consider a discrete Gaussian distribution with respect to a lattice. The Gaussian function centered in a vector $\mathbf{c}$ with parameter $s > 0$ is defined as $\rho_{s,\mathbf{c}}(\mathbf{x}) = e^{-\pi\|(\mathbf{x}-\mathbf{c})/s\|^2}$. The corresponding probability density function proportional to $\rho_{s,\mathbf{c}}$ is defined as $D_{s,\mathbf{c}}(\mathbf{x}) = \rho_{s,\mathbf{c}}(\mathbf{x})/s^n$ for all $\mathbf{x} \in \mathbb{R}^n$. With respect to a lattice Λ the discrete Gaussian distribution is defined as $D_{\Lambda,s,\mathbf{c}}(\mathbf{x}) = D_{s,\mathbf{c}}(\mathbf{x})/D_{s,\mathbf{c}}(\Lambda) = \rho_{s,\mathbf{c}}(\mathbf{x})/\rho_{s,\mathbf{c}}(\Lambda)$ for all $\mathbf{x} \in \Lambda$. Since $\mathbb{Z}^m$ is also a lattice, we can define a discrete Gaussian distribution for $\mathbb{Z}^m$. By $D_{\mathbb{Z}^m,\sigma}$, we denote the discrete Gaussian distribution for $\mathbb{Z}^m$ around the origin with the standard deviation σ.

2.3　Lattice-Related Computational Problems

The security of our scheme relies on the hardness of the two lattice-based problems defined below.

Learning with Errors (LWE)

Definition 1. *Learning With Errors (LWE) [23] is parametrized by integers $n, m \geq 1$, and $q \geq 2$. For a vector $s \in \mathbb{Z}_q^n$ and χ, the distribution $A_{s,\chi}$ is obtained by sampling $a \in \mathbb{Z}_q^n$ uniformly at random and choosing $e \leftarrow \chi$, and outputting the pair $(\mathbf{a}, \mathbf{a}^T \cdot \mathbf{s} + e)$.*

There are two LWE problems: Search-LWE and Decision-LWE. While Search-LWE is to find the secret $\mathbf{s}$ given LWE samples, Decision-LWE is to distinguish LWE samples and samples chosen according to the uniformly distribution. We use the hardness of Decision-LWE problem.

For a prime power q, $b \geq \sqrt{n}\omega(\log n)$, and distribution χ, solving $LWE_{n,q,\chi}$ problem is at least as hard as solving $SIVP_\gamma$ (*Shortest Independent Vector Problem*), where $\gamma = \tilde{O}(nq/b)$ [27].

Short Integer Solution ($\text{SIS}_{n,m,q,\beta}$)

Definition 2. *Short Integer Solution ($SIS_{n,m,q,\beta}$ [23,27]) is as follows. Given m uniformly random vectors $a_i \in \mathbb{Z}_q^n$, forming the columns of a matrix $\mathbf{A} \in \mathbb{Z}_q^{n \times m}$, find a nonzero vector $\mathbf{x} \in \mathbb{Z}^m$ such that $||\mathbf{x}|| \leq \beta$ and $\mathbf{A}\mathbf{x} = 0 \bmod q$.*

For any m, $\beta = \mathsf{poly}(n)$, and for any $q \geq \sqrt{n}\beta$, solving $SIS_{n,m,q,\beta}$ problem with non-negligible probability is at least as hard as solving $SIVP_\gamma$ problem, for some $\gamma = \tilde{O}(\beta\sqrt{n})$ [15].

2.4　Lattice-Related Algorithms

Lemma 1 ([9, Lemma 2.3]). *GPVSample is a PPT (probabilistic polynomial-time) algorithm that takes a basis $\mathbf{B}$ of a lattice $\Lambda \subseteq \mathbb{Z}^n$ and $s \geq ||\tilde{\mathbf{B}}||.\Omega(\sqrt{\log n})$ as inputs, and outputs vectors $\mathbf{b} \in \Lambda$ with distribution $D_{\Lambda,s}$.*

Lemma 2 ([2, Theorem 3.2]). *TrapGen is a PPT algorithm that takes $1^n, 1^m$ and an integer $q \geq 2$, where $m \geq \Omega(n \log q)$ as inputs, and outputs a matrix $\mathbf{A} \in \mathbb{Z}_q^{n \times m}$ and a basis $\mathbf{T_A}$ of $\Lambda_q^\perp(\mathbf{A})$. The distribution of the output $\mathbf{A}$ is within statistical distance $2^{-\Omega(n)}$ to $U(\mathbb{Z}_q^{n \times m})$, and $||\widetilde{\mathbf{T_A}}|| \leq \mathcal{O}(\sqrt{n \log q})$.*

Lemma 3 ([13, Lemma 3.2]). *ExtBasis is a PPT algorithm that takes a matrix $\mathbf{B} \in \mathbb{Z}_q^{n \times m'}$, whose first m columns span $\mathbb{Z}_q^n$, and a basis $\mathbf{T_A}$ of $\Lambda_q^\perp(\mathbf{A})$, where $\mathbf{A}$ is the left $n \times m$ submatrix of $\mathbf{B}$ as inputs, and outputs a basis $\mathbf{T_B}$ of $\Lambda_q^\perp(\mathbf{B})$ with $||\widetilde{\mathbf{T_B}}|| \leq ||\widetilde{\mathbf{T_A}}||$.*

Lemma 4 ([1, Theorem 3]). *SampleRight is a PPT algorithm that takes matrices $\boldsymbol{A}, \boldsymbol{C} \in \mathbb{Z}_q^{n \times m}$, a low-norm matrix $\boldsymbol{R} \in \mathbb{Z}^{m \times m}$, a short basis $\boldsymbol{T_C} \in \mathbb{Z}^{m \times m}$ of $\Lambda_q^\perp(\boldsymbol{C})$, a vector $\boldsymbol{u} \in \mathbb{Z}_q^n$ and a rational s such that $s \geq ||\widetilde{\boldsymbol{T}_C}|| \cdot \Omega(\sqrt{\log n})$ as inputs, and outputs vectors $\boldsymbol{b} \in \mathbb{Z}^{2m}$, such that $[\boldsymbol{A} \mid \boldsymbol{A} \cdot \boldsymbol{R} + \boldsymbol{C}] \cdot \boldsymbol{b} = \boldsymbol{u} \mod q$ and with distribution statistically close to $D_{\Lambda,s}$, where Λ denotes the shifted lattice $\{\boldsymbol{x} \in \mathbb{Z}^{2m} : [\boldsymbol{A} \mid \boldsymbol{A} \cdot \boldsymbol{R} + \boldsymbol{C}] \cdot \boldsymbol{x} = \boldsymbol{u} \mod q\}.$*

3   Coping with VLR for Libert's Dynamic Group Signature Scheme from Lattices

This section first recalls the scheme given in [20] in brief, which used the syntax and security model of Kiayias and Yung [18]. Then this section discusses the complications of incorporating VLR with the group signature schemes based on lattices and how to achieve the problems with a justified scheme.

The "power-of-2" matrix $\mathbf{H}_{n \times n \lceil \log q \rceil} \in \mathbb{Z}_q^{n \times n \lceil \log q \rceil}$, for any positive integers n, and $q \geq 2$ is given as

$$\mathbf{H}_{n \times n \lceil \log q \rceil} = \mathbf{I}_n \otimes [1 \,|\, 2 \,|\, 4 \,|\, \ldots \,|\, 2^{\lceil \log q \rceil - 1}] =$$
$$\begin{bmatrix} 1\,2\,4\ldots 2^{\lceil \log q \rceil - 1} & & & \\ & 1\,2\,4\ldots 2^{\lceil \log q \rceil - 1} & & \\ & & \ddots & \\ & & & 1\,2\,4\ldots 2^{\lceil \log q \rceil - 1} \end{bmatrix}.$$

Moreover, for each vector $\mathbf{v} = \mathbf{H}_{n \times n \lceil \log q \rceil} \cdot \mathsf{bin}(\mathbf{v}) \in \mathbb{Z}_q^n$, where $\mathsf{bin}(\mathbf{v}) \in \{0,1\}^{n \lceil \log q \rceil}$ is the binary expression of $\mathbf{v}$ and $\mathsf{bin}(\mathbf{v})$ is obtained by replacing each coordinate of $\mathbf{v}$.

The key component of the scheme given in [20] is the two-message joining protocol. Through the joining-protocol, new users can join the group and the group manager can grant the member certifications. First new user $User_i$, who is having a long-term public and private key pair ($\mathsf{upk}[i]$ and $\mathsf{usk}[i]$) samples a secret signing key $\mathbf{x}_i \hookleftarrow D_{\mathbb{Z}^{4m}, \sigma}$, which is a short vector and used to compute a syndrome $\mathbf{v}_i = \mathbf{F} \cdot \mathbf{x}_i \in \mathbb{Z}_q^{4n}$ (where $m = 2n \lceil \log q \rceil$ and $\mathbf{F} \in \mathbb{Z}_q^{4n \times 4m}$). The group manager signs $\mathsf{bin}(\mathbf{v}_i)$ the binary expression of $\mathbf{v}_i$ to generate the certification. Finally, the group manager sends the triple $(id_i, \mathbf{d}_i, \mathbf{s}_i)$ to the new user $User_i$, where id_i is the ℓ-bit identifier selected for the new user and $\mathbf{d}_i$ is the computed short vector using the sampled short vector $\mathbf{s}_i$. The user $User_i$ can sign a message with his secret signing key $\mathbf{x}_i$ and his member certificate $(id_i, \mathbf{d}_i, \mathbf{s}_i)$. By using a Stern-like protocol, $User_i$ can prove he has a valid certificate, which is associated with the public key $\mathbf{v}_i$.

However, when applying Verifier-local revocation method to a scheme and trying to achieve full-security, two main points should be take care. (1) The revocation tokens (especially the challenged indices' tokens) should not be given to the adversary since he can execute Verify with those tokens and identify the signer of the challenging signature. (2) The revocation tokens should not be a part of the secret signing key. Since at the full-anonymity defined in the BMW03 model, the almost-full anonymity defined in [25], and the dynamical-almost-full anonymity given in [24], all the secret signing keys are given to the adversary, and the adversary can extract the revocation tokens from the secret signing keys easily if we generate revocation token as a part of the secret signing key. When we apply VLR to the scheme in [20], we can use the almost-full anonymity given in [25] as a solution for the case (1). The almost-full anonymity provides all the secret signing keys and the group public key to the adversary at the beginning of the game as in the full-anonymity game [4]. But, the revocation tokens are given only upon the request of the adversary. Moreover, revocation tokens are not provided, which are used for generating the challenging signature, and the challenging signature is not generated for the indices, whose revocation tokens are revealed. Then we use a vector $\mathbf{d}_i$ to make the revocation token of the new scheme. Since $\mathbf{d}_i$ should satisfy some computation with $\mathrm{bin}(\mathbf{v}_i)$ and some other parameters, it has a connection to the identifier and the public key of the signer. Hence, the signers cannot forge $\mathbf{d}_i$. Accordingly, $\mathbf{d}_i$ is suitable for the revocation token. Moreover, for member revocation, the group manager should know the revocation token of the revoking member. Since $\mathbf{d}_i$ is generated by the group manager he can create the revocation token and provide with the member certificate. Using $\mathbf{d}_i$ for creating revocation token is suitable and it is the solution for the concern (2).

Moreover, when dealing with fully dynamic group signature scheme with member registration, we should allow the adversary to join the group as a new member. At the joining protocol, the group manager provides the certification including the revocation token to the new users. By using this information, the adversary can attack later at the challenging phase. The dynamical-almost-full anonymity suggested in [24] which is an extended version of the almost-full anonymity for fully-dynamic group signature schemes provides a solution for this matter. In the dynamical-almost-full anonymity, when the adversary joins the group as a new user, the revocation token will not be provided. However, the adversary can request any revocation token (including newly added ones) except revocation tokens of the indices used to generate challenging signature (as in the almost-full anonymity). Moreover, at the challenging phase, the adversary can only use the indices which are added by him at the registration query. Thus, the adversary cannot cheat using the user details added before the game as a legal member.

The dynamical-almost-full anonymity game between a challenger C and an adversary A is as below.

- **Initial Phase:** The challenger C runs KeyGen to obtain a group public key **gpk**, authorities' secret keys (**ik**, **ok**). Then gives **gpk** and existing group members' secret signing keys **gsk** to the adversary A.
- **Query Phase:** A can join the group as a new user any number of time via registration query. C generates revocation token and certificate for the new user if the new user is valid. Then C saves the new user's information in

reg. However, C will not provide the revocation token of the newly added user to A at the time of registering. Thus, member certification *cert* is sent without the revocation token. Moreover, A can query revocation token (**grt**) of any user and can access the opening oracle with any message M and a valid signature Σ.

- **Challenge Phase:** A outputs a message M^* and two distinct identities i_0, i_1. If revocation tokens of i_0, i_1 were not revealed by A and if i_0, i_1 are indices of newly added users by A, then C selects a bit $b \xleftarrow{\$} \{0,1\}$, generates $\Sigma^* =$ Sign(**gpk**, **gsk**$[i_b]$, *cert*$_{i_b}$, M^*), and sends Σ^* to A. A still can query the opening oracle except the signature challenged and revocation queries except using the challenged indices. A can add users to the group as before.

- **Guessing Phase:** Finally, A outputs a bit b', the guess of b. If $b' = b$, then A wins.

Our scheme uses the dynamical-almost-full anonymity to ensure the security.

4 New Scheme

The construction of the new scheme is same as the dynamic lattice-based group signature scheme suggested in [20], but with member revocation facility using VLR. Thus, the group manager can revoke misbehaved members other than providing member certifications. In such a way, our scheme offers both member registration and member revocation. However, we present our scheme by highlighting the differences between our scheme and the scheme given in [20].

Our scheme consists of six algorithms; Setup, Join, Sign, Verify, Open, and Revoke. In the beginning, the group public key and the authority keys are generated in Setup. A new user, who wants to join the group should interact with the group manager using Join. If the key provided by the new user is valid, then the group manager issues the member certification. In the scheme given in [20], the member certification is $(id_i, \mathbf{d}_i, \mathbf{s}_i)$, where id_i is the identifier of the new member, and $\mathbf{d}_i$ and $\mathbf{s}_i$ are short vectors. Here we use the short vector $\mathbf{d}_i$ to generate the new member's revocation token $\mathbf{grt}[i] = \mathbf{A} \cdot \mathbf{r}_i$, where $\mathbf{r}_i$ is an element of $\mathbf{d}_i$. Thus, member certification issued by the group manager will be $(id_i, \mathbf{d}_i, \mathbf{s}_i, \mathbf{grt}[i])$ in our scheme. When a member wants to generate a signature, he has to compute $\mathbf{v} = \mathbf{V} \cdot (\mathbf{A} \cdot \mathbf{r}_i) + \mathbf{e}_1 \mod q$ other than the computations given in [20]. At the verification stage of the signature (in Verify), the verifiers check the validity of the signer by screening the revocation list he has. Authenticating the signer is not given in [20] because they have not considered the member revocation. We use the algorithms Setup and Open given in [20] without any change. However, we provide a new algorithm called Revoke to cancel the membership of the misbehaved members.

4.1 Description of Our Scheme

Setup: The randomized algorithm KeyGen($1^n, 1^m$) works as follows.

1. Run $\mathsf{TrapGen}(1^n, 1^m, q)$ to get $\mathbf{A} \in \mathbb{Z}_q^{n \times m}$ and a short basis $\mathbf{T_A}$. Then sample random matrices $\mathbf{A}_0, \mathbf{A}_1, \ldots, \mathbf{A}_\ell, \mathbf{D} \hookleftarrow U(\mathbb{Z}_q^{n \times m}), \mathbf{D}_0, \mathbf{D}_1 \hookleftarrow U(\mathbb{Z}_q^{2n \times 2m})$ and a vector $\mathbf{u} \hookleftarrow U(\mathbb{Z}_q^n)$.
2. Select an additional random matrix $\mathbf{F} \hookleftarrow U(\mathbb{Z}_q^{4n \times 4m})$.
3. Generate a master key pair; a statistically uniform matrix $\mathbf{B} \in \mathbb{Z}_q^{n \times m}$ and a short basis $\mathbf{T_B} \in \mathbb{Z}^{m \times m}$ for the GPV-IBE [15] scheme in its multi-bit variant. The basis $\mathbf{T_B}$ allows to compute GPV private keys with a Gaussian parameter $\sigma_{GPV} \geq \|\widetilde{\mathbf{T_B}}\| \cdot \sqrt{\log m}$.
4. Choose a one-time signature scheme $\mathcal{OTS} = (\mathsf{OGen}, \mathsf{OSign}, \mathsf{OVer})$, and a hash function $\mathcal{H}_0 : \{0,1\}^* \to \mathbb{Z}_q^{n \times 2m}$.
5. Finally, we have the group public key $\mathbf{gpk} := (\mathbf{A}, \{\mathbf{A}_j\}_{j=0}^\ell, \mathbf{B}, \mathbf{D}, \mathbf{D}_0, \mathbf{D}_1, \mathbf{F}, \mathbf{u}, \mathcal{OTS}, \mathcal{H}, \mathcal{H}_0)$, the group manager's (issuer's) secret key $\mathbf{ik} := \mathbf{T_A}$ and the opener's secret key $\mathbf{ok} := \mathbf{T_B}$.

Join: A new user $User_i$, who has a personal public and private key pair $(\mathbf{upk}[i], \mathbf{usk}[i] \leftarrow \mathsf{UKg}(1^n))$ interacts with the group manager GM to join the group through the joining protocol.

1. $User_i$ samples a discrete Gaussian vector $\mathbf{x}_i \leftarrow D_{\mathbb{Z}^{4m}, \sigma}$, and computes $\mathbf{z}_i \leftarrow \mathbf{F} \cdot \mathbf{x}_i \in \mathbb{Z}_q^{4n}$, where $\mathbf{x}_i$ is the secret signing key ($\mathbf{gsk}[i]$) of $User_i$. Then he generates an ordinary digital signature $\Sigma_{join} \leftarrow \mathsf{Sig}(\mathbf{usk}[i], \mathbf{z}_i)$, whose binary representation $\mathsf{bin}(\mathbf{z}_i)$ consists of $4n\lceil \log q \rceil = 2m$ bits, and sends $\mathbf{z}_i$ and Σ_{join} to the group manager GM.
2. The group manager verifies that $\mathbf{z}_i$ was not previously used by any user using the registration table reg and he verifies Σ_{join} is a valid signature on $\mathbf{z}_i$, using $\mathsf{Vf}(\mathbf{upk}[i], \mathbf{z}_i, \Sigma_{join})$. He aborts if any condition fails. Otherwise, the group manager selects a fresh ℓ-bit string $id_i = id_i[1] \ldots id_i[\ell] \in \{0,1\}^\ell$ as the index of the user $User_i$. Then GM certifies the new user $User_i$ as a new member and generates the member certification as below.
First, GM defines a matrix for $User_i$,

$$\mathbf{A}_{id_i} = \left[\mathbf{A} \mid \mathbf{A}_0 + \sum_{j=1}^\ell id_i[j] \mathbf{A}_j \right] \in \mathbb{Z}_q^{n \times 2m}. \tag{1}$$

Next, GM executes $\mathsf{ExtBasis}(\mathbf{A}_{id_i}, \mathbf{T_A})$ to obtain a short delegated basis $\mathbf{T}'_{id_i}$ of $\Lambda_q^\perp(\mathbf{A}_{id_i}) \in \mathbb{Z}^{2m \times 2m}$.
Then, GM choses a short vector $\mathbf{s}_i \hookleftarrow D_{\mathbb{Z}^{2m}, \sigma}$, and uses delegated basis $\mathbf{T}'_{id_i}$ to compute short vector $\mathbf{d}_i = \begin{bmatrix} \mathbf{d}_{i,1} \\ \mathbf{d}_{i,2} \end{bmatrix} \in \mathbb{Z}^{2m}$ such that

$$\mathbf{A}_{id_i} \mathbf{d}_i = \left[\mathbf{A} \mid \mathbf{A}_0 + \sum_{j=1}^\ell id_i[j] \mathbf{A}_j \right] \cdot \mathbf{d}_i$$
$$= \mathbf{u} + \mathbf{D} \cdot \mathsf{bin}(\mathbf{D}_0 \cdot \mathsf{bin}(\mathbf{z}_i) + \mathbf{D}_1 \cdot \mathbf{s}_i) \bmod q. \tag{2}$$

After that, GM selects $\mathbf{d}_{i,1}$ or $\mathbf{d}_{i,2}$ randomly as $\mathbf{r}_i$ and generates the revocation token $\mathbf{grt}[i] = (\mathbf{A} \cdot \mathbf{r}_i)$ and member certification $cert_i = (id_i, \mathbf{d}_i, \mathbf{s}_i, \mathbf{grt}[i])$.

Finally, GM saves the new member's details $(\mathbf{z}_i, cert_i, i, \mathbf{upk}[i], \Sigma_{join})$ and sends the certification $cert_i = (id_i, \mathbf{d}_i, \mathbf{s}_i, \mathbf{grt}[i])$ to the new user.

Sign: $\mathsf{Sign}(\mathbf{gpk}, \mathbf{gsk}[i], cert_i, M)$ is a randomized algorithm, that generates a signature Σ on a given message M using $\mathbf{gsk} = \mathbf{x}_i \in \mathbb{Z}^{4m}$ and $cert_i$ as follows.

1. Parse $cert_i$ as $(id_i, \mathbf{d}_i, \mathbf{s}_i, \mathbf{grt}[i])$, where $\mathbf{d}_i = [\mathbf{d}_{i,1}^T | \mathbf{d}_{i,2}^T]^T \in \mathbb{Z}^{2m}$, $\mathbf{s}_i \in \mathbb{Z}^{2m}$ and $\mathbf{grt}[i] = (\mathbf{A} \cdot \mathbf{r}_i)$.
2. Generate one-time signature key pair as $\mathsf{OGen}(1^n) \to (\mathbf{ovk}, \mathbf{osk})$.
3. Encrypt the index $d = \mathsf{bin}(\mathbf{z}_i)$, where $\mathbf{z}_i = \mathbf{F} \cdot \mathbf{x}_i$ and compute $\mathbf{c}_{\mathbf{z}_i} \in \mathbb{Z}_q^m \times \mathbb{Z}_q^{2m}$.
   (a) Let $\mathbf{G} = \mathcal{H}_0(\mathbf{ovk}) \in \mathbb{Z}_q^{n \times 2m}$.
   (b) Sample $\mathbf{e}_0 \leftarrow \chi^n$, $\mathbf{e}_1 \leftarrow \chi^m$ and $\mathbf{e}_2 \leftarrow \chi^{2m}$.
   (c) Compute the ciphertext $\mathbf{c}_{\mathbf{z}_i}$

$$\mathbf{c}_{\mathbf{z}_i} = (\mathbf{c}_1, \mathbf{c}_2) = (\mathbf{B}^T \mathbf{e}_0 + \mathbf{e}_1, \mathbf{G}^T \mathbf{e}_0 + \mathbf{e}_2 + \mathsf{bin}(\mathbf{z}_i)\lfloor q/2 \rfloor). \quad (3)$$

4. Sample $\rho \xleftarrow{\$} \{0,1\}^n$, let $\mathbf{V} = \mathcal{G}(\mathbf{A}, \mathbf{u}, M, \rho) \in \mathbb{Z}_q^{m \times n}$ and compute $\mathbf{v} = \mathbf{V} \cdot (\mathbf{A} \cdot \mathbf{r}_i) + \mathbf{e}_1 \bmod q$ ($\mathcal{G} : \{0,1\}^* \to \mathbb{Z}_q^{n \times m}$ is a random oracle and $\|\mathbf{e}_1\|_\infty \le \beta$ with overwhelming probability).
5. Use the protocol given in Sect. 4.2 to prove the knowledge of $id_i \in \{0,1\}^\ell$, vectors $\mathbf{s}_i \in \mathbb{Z}^{2m}, \mathbf{d}_{i,1}, \mathbf{d}_{i,2} \in \mathbb{Z}^m, \mathbf{x}_i \in \mathbb{Z}^{4m}$ with infinity norm bound β; $\mathbf{e}_0 \in \chi^n, \mathbf{e}_1 \in \chi^m, \mathbf{e}_2 \in \chi^{2m}$ with infinity norm bound b and $\mathsf{bin}(\mathbf{z}_i) \in \{0,1\}^{2m}, \mathbf{w}_i \in \{0,1\}^m$, that satisfy Eq. (3) and

$$\mathbf{A} \cdot \mathbf{d}_{i,1} + \mathbf{A}_0 \cdot \mathbf{d}_{i,2} + \sum_{j=1}^{\ell} (id_i[j] \cdot \mathbf{d}_{i,2}) \cdot \mathbf{A}_j - \mathbf{D} \cdot \mathbf{w}_i = \mathbf{u} \in \mathbb{Z}_q^n \text{ and}$$

$$\begin{cases} \mathbf{H}_{2n \times m} \cdot \mathbf{w}_i = \mathbf{D}_0 \cdot \mathsf{bin}(\mathbf{z}_i) + \mathbf{D}_1 \cdot \mathbf{s}_i \in \mathbb{Z}_q^{2n} \\ \mathbf{F} \cdot \mathbf{x}_i = \mathbf{H}_{4n \times 2m} \cdot \mathsf{bin}(\mathbf{z}_i) \in \mathbb{Z}_q^{4n} \\ \mathbf{V} \cdot (\mathbf{A} \cdot \mathbf{r}_i) + \mathbf{e}_1 = \mathbf{v} \bmod q. \end{cases}$$

Repeat the protocol $t = \omega(\log n)$ times to make the soundness error negligible. Then make it non-interactive using the Fiat-Shamir heuristic as a triple, $\Pi = (\{CMT^{(k)}\}_{k=1}^t, CH, \{RSP^{(k)}\}_{k=1}^t)$, where $CH = (\{Ch^{(k)}\}_{k=1}^t) = \mathcal{H}(M, \mathbf{ovk}, \{CMT^{(k)}\}_{k=1}^t, \mathbf{c}_{\mathbf{z}_i})$.
6. Compute one-time signature $sig = \mathsf{OSig}(\mathbf{osk}, (\mathbf{c}_{\mathbf{z}_i}, \Pi))$.
7. Output signature $\Sigma = (\mathbf{ovk}, \mathbf{c}_{\mathbf{z}_i}, \Pi, sig, \mathbf{v}, \rho)$.

Verify: The deterministic algorithm $\mathsf{Verify}(\mathbf{gpk}, M, \Sigma, RL)$, where $RL = \{\{\mathbf{u}_i\}_i\}$ works as follows.

1. Parse the signature Σ as $(\mathbf{ovk}, \mathbf{c}_{\mathbf{z}_i}, \Pi, sig, \mathbf{v}, \rho)$.
2. Get $\mathbf{V} = \mathcal{G}(\mathbf{A}, \mathbf{u}, M, \rho) \in \mathbb{Z}_q^{m \times n}$.
3. If $\mathsf{OVer}(\mathbf{ovk}, (\mathbf{c}_{\mathbf{z}_i}, \Pi), sig) = 0$ then return 0.
4. Parse Π as $(\{CMT^{(k)}\}_{k=1}^t, \{Ch^{(k)}\}_{k=1}^t, \{RSP^{(k)}\}_{k=1}^t)$.
5. If $(Ch^{(1)}, \dots, Ch^{(t)}) \ne \mathcal{H}(M, \{CMT^{(k)}\}_{k=1}^t, \mathbf{c}_1, \mathbf{c}_2)$ return 0 else proceed.
6. For $k = 1$ to t run the verification steps of the commitment scheme to validate $RSP^{(k)}$ with respect to $CMT^{(k)}$ and $Ch^{(k)}$. If any of the conditions fails then output invalid.

7. For each $\mathbf{u}_i \in RL$ compute $\mathbf{e}'_j = \mathbf{v} - \mathbf{V} \cdot \mathbf{u}_i \bmod q$ to check whether there exists an index i such that $\|\mathbf{e}_i\|_\infty \leq \beta$. If so return invalid.
8. Return valid.

Open: Open(**gpk**, **ok**, M, Σ, reg) functions as below.

1. Parse $\mathbf{ok} = \mathbf{T_B}$ and Σ as $(\mathbf{ovk}, \mathbf{c}_{\mathbf{z}_i}, \Pi, sig, \mathbf{v}, \rho)$.
2. Let $\mathbf{G} = \mathcal{H}_0(\mathbf{ovk}) \in \mathbb{Z}_q^{n \times 2m}$.
3. Using $\mathbf{T_B}$ compute a small norm matrix $\mathbf{Y} \in \mathbb{Z}^{m \times 2m}$, where $\mathbf{B} \cdot \mathbf{Y} = \mathbf{G} \bmod q$.
4. Compute $\mathbf{bin}(\mathbf{z}) = \lfloor (\mathbf{c}_2 - \mathbf{Y}^T \cdot \mathbf{c}_1)/(q/2) \rceil$.
5. Determine whether the obtained $\mathbf{bin}(\mathbf{z})$ is corresponding to a vector $\mathbf{z} = \mathbf{H}_{4n \times 2m} \cdot \mathbf{bin}(\mathbf{z}) \bmod q$ in reg and output the corresponding index i.

Revoke: The algorithm Revoke(**gpk**, **ik**, i, reg) functions as follows.

1. Query reg for i and obtain revoking member's revocation token $(\mathbf{A} \cdot \mathbf{r}_i)$.
2. Add $(\mathbf{A} \cdot \mathbf{r}_i)$ to RL and update the registration table $reg[i]$ to inactive (0).
3. Return RL and reg.

4.2 The Underlying ZKAoK for the Group Signature Scheme

Let COM be the statistically hiding and computationally binding commitment scheme described in [17]. The common inputs are matrices $\mathbf{A}, \mathbf{A}_0, \mathbf{A}_1, \ldots, \mathbf{A}_\ell, \mathbf{D}, \mathbf{B} \in \mathbb{Z}_q^{n \times m}, \mathbf{D}_0, \mathbf{D}_1 \in \mathbb{Z}_q^{2n \times 2m}, \mathbf{F} \in \mathbb{Z}_q^{4n \times 4m}, \mathbf{H}_{2n \times m} \in \mathbb{Z}_q^{2n \times m}, \mathbf{H}_{4n \times 2m} \in \mathbb{Z}_q^{4n \times 2m}, \mathbf{G} \in \mathbb{Z}^{n \times 2m}, \mathbf{V} \in \mathbb{Z}^{m \times n}$ and vectors $\mathbf{u} \in \mathbb{Z}_q^n, \mathbf{c}_1 \in \mathbb{Z}_q^m, \mathbf{c}_2 \in \mathbb{Z}_q^{2m}, \mathbf{v} \in \mathbb{Z}_q^n$. The prover's inputs are $\mathbf{x} \in [-\beta, \beta]^{4m}, \mathbf{y} \in \{0,1\}^{2m}, \mathbf{w} \in \{0,1\}^m, \mathbf{d}_1, \mathbf{d}_2 \in [-\beta, \beta]^m, \mathbf{s} \in [-\beta, \beta]^{2m}, id = (id[1], \ldots, id[\ell])^T \in \{0,1\}^\ell, \mathbf{e}_0 \in [-b, b]^n, \mathbf{e}_1 \in [-b, b]^m, \mathbf{e}_2 \in [-b, b]^{2m}, \mathbf{r} \in [-\beta, \beta]^m$. The prover's goal is to convince the verifier in ZK that

$$\begin{cases} \mathbf{F} \cdot \mathbf{x} = \mathbf{H}_{4n \times 2m} \cdot \mathbf{y} \bmod q; \mathbf{H}_{2n \times m} \cdot \mathbf{w} = \mathbf{D}_0 \cdot \mathbf{y} + \mathbf{D}_1 \cdot \mathbf{s} \bmod q; \\ \mathbf{A} \cdot \mathbf{d}_1 + \mathbf{A}_0 \cdot \mathbf{d}_2 + \sum_{j=1}^\ell \mathbf{A}_j \cdot (id[j] \cdot \mathbf{d}_2) - \mathbf{D} \cdot \mathbf{w} = \mathbf{u} \bmod q; \\ \mathbf{c}_1 = \mathbf{B}^T \mathbf{e}_0 + \mathbf{e}_1 \bmod q; \mathbf{c}_2 = \mathbf{G}^T \mathbf{e}_0 + \mathbf{e}_2 + \lfloor q/2 \rfloor \cdot \mathbf{y} \bmod q; \\ \mathbf{V} \cdot (\mathbf{A} \cdot \mathbf{r}) + \mathbf{e}_1 = \mathbf{v} \bmod q. \end{cases}$$

We use the interacting protocol given in [20]. To prove $\mathbf{V} \cdot (\mathbf{A} \cdot \mathbf{r}) + \mathbf{e}_1 = \mathbf{v} \bmod q$ we use the proof given in [26].

5 Correctness and Security Analysis of the Scheme

5.1 Correctness

1. Assume both the group manager and the new user follow the joining protocol honestly and communicate via a secured channel. The group manager verifies whether the public key of the new user is not being used before, and issues the member-certificate with revocation token only for valid users.

2. For all **gpk**, **gsk**, and **grt**,
   $\mathsf{Verify}(\mathbf{gpk}, M, \mathsf{Sign}(\mathbf{gpk}, \mathbf{gsk}[i], (id_i, \mathbf{d}_i, \mathbf{s}_i, \mathbf{grt}[i]), M), RL) = \text{Valid and}$
   $\mathbf{grt}[i] \notin RL.$
   $\mathsf{Open}(\mathbf{gpk}, \mathbf{ok}, M, \mathsf{Sign}(\mathbf{gpk}, \mathbf{gsk}[i], (id_i, \mathbf{d}_i, \mathbf{s}_i, \mathbf{grt}[i]), M), reg) = i.$

Verify in the proposed scheme only accepts signatures generated on given messages and which are only generated by active (not revoked) and honest users (has member certificate). If the revocation token of the signer is in RL, then his signature is not accepted by Verify. Similarly Sign also checks whether the signer can satisfy those requirements. The signer has to convince the verifier his validity using the zero-knowledge protocol. Zero-knowledge protocol guarantees no one can sign and pass the verification of signing process without having a valid membership and secret signing key. The algorithm Open outputs the index of the signer with overwhelming probability. It computes $\mathsf{bin}(\mathbf{z}_i)$ and verifies with the registration table reg.

5.2   Anonymity

Theorem 1. *In the random oracle model, the proposed scheme is dynamical-almost-full anonymous based on the hardness of $Decision - LWE_{n,q,\chi}$ problem.*

Here a sequence of games between the challenger and the adversary is used, where the advantage of the adversary is negligible in the last game.

Game 0: This is the real experiment. The challenger C runs $\mathsf{KeyGen}(1^n, 1^N)$ to obtain the group public key and the authorities' keys. The challenger C gives the group public key **gpk** and all the existing group members' secret keys **gsk** to the adversary A. However any revocation token information is not given to A at the beginning. In the query phase, A can join as a new member any number of time through the registration query. In the registration query, C will accept valid members but will provide the certification $cert = (id_i, \varepsilon, \mathbf{s}_i, \varepsilon)$ without new user's revocation token or related details. However, A can request for revocation tokens of any member, and he can access opening query for any signature. In the challenge phase, A sends two indices (i_0, i_1) together with a message M^*. If (i_0, i_1) are newly added by A and if (i_0, i_1) are not used for querying revocation tokens, then C generates and sends back the challenging signature $\Sigma^* = (\mathbf{ovk}^*, \mathbf{c}_{\mathbf{z}_i}^*, \Pi^*, sig^*, \mathbf{v}^*, \rho^*)$ for a random bit $b \leftarrow \{0, 1\}$. The adversary's goal is to identify which index is used to generate the challenging signature. A returns b'. If $b' = b$ then the experiment returns 1. Otherwise, returns 0.

Game 1: In this game, the challenger C makes a slight modification with respect to Game 0. In real experiment (Game 0) one-time key pair $(\mathbf{ovk}, \mathbf{osk})$ is generated at the signature generation. In this game, C generates the one-time key pair $(\mathbf{ovk}^*, \mathbf{osk}^*)$ at the beginning of the game. If the adversary A accesses the opening oracle with a valid signature $\Sigma = (\mathbf{ovk}, \mathbf{c}_{\mathbf{z}_i}, \Pi, sig, \mathbf{v}, \rho)$, where $\mathbf{ovk} = \mathbf{ovk}^*$, C returns a random bit and aborts. However, A comes up with a signature Σ, where $\mathbf{ovk} = \mathbf{ovk}^*$ contradicts the strong unforgeability of $\mathcal{OTS}$, and since $\mathbf{ovk}^*$ is independent of the adversary's view, probability of

$\mathbf{ovk} = \mathbf{ovk}^*$ is negligible. Even after seeing the challenging signature if A comes up with a valid signature $\Sigma = (\mathbf{ovk}, \mathbf{c}_{\mathbf{z}_i}, \Pi, sig, \mathbf{v}, \rho)$, where $\mathbf{ovk} = \mathbf{ovk}^*$, then sig is a forged one-time signature, which defeats the strong unforgeability of $\mathcal{OTS}$. Thus, we assume that A does not request for opening of a valid signature with $\mathbf{ovk}^*$ and the challenger aborting the game is negligible.

Game 2: The challenger C programs the random oracle $\mathcal{H}_0$. At the beginning of the game, C replaces $\mathbf{G}$. C chooses uniformly random matrix $\mathbf{G}^* \in \mathbb{Z}_q^{n \times 2m}$ and sets $\mathcal{H}_0(\mathbf{ovk}^*) = \mathbf{G}^*$. To answer the opening oracle requests of A with $\Sigma = (\mathbf{ovk}, \mathbf{c}_{\mathbf{z}_i}, \Pi, sig, \mathbf{v}, \rho)$, C samples a small-norm matrix $\mathbf{Y} \leftarrow D^{2m}_{\mathbb{Z}^{2m}, \sigma}$, and computes $\mathbf{G} = \mathbf{B} \cdot \mathbf{Y} \bmod q$. This $\mathbf{G}$ is used to answer the signature openings in later and keep track of $(\mathbf{ovk}, \mathbf{Y}, \mathbf{G})$ to be reused if A repeats the same requests for $\mathcal{H}_0(\mathbf{ovk})$. Since for the view of A, the distribution of $\mathbf{G}^*$ is statistically close to the real experiment [15], Game 2 is indistinguishable from Game 1.

Game 3: Instead of honestly generating the legitimate non-interactive proof Π, the challenger C simulates the proof without using the witness. C invokes the simulator for each $k \in [t]$ and then programs the random oracle $\mathcal{H}$ accordingly. The challenging signature $\Sigma^* = (\mathbf{ovk}^*, \mathbf{c}_{\mathbf{z}_i}^*, \Pi^*, sig^*, \mathbf{v}^*, \rho^*)$ is statistically close to the challenging signature in Game 2 because the argument system is statistically zero-knowledge. Thus Game 3 is indistinguishable from Game 2.

Game 4: Here, the challenger C replaces the original revocation token by a vector $\mathbf{t} \overset{\$}{\leftarrow} \mathbb{Z}_q^n$ sampled uniformly random. The original game has $\mathbf{v} = \mathbf{V} \cdot \mathbf{grt}[i_b] + \mathbf{e}_1 \bmod q$. In this game, $\mathbf{v} = \mathbf{V} \cdot \mathbf{t} + \mathbf{e}_1 \bmod q$, where $\mathbf{V}$ is uniformly random over $\mathbb{Z}_q^{m \times n}$, $\mathbf{e}_1$ is sampled from the error distribution χ. C replaces only the revocation token $\mathbf{grt}[i_b]$ with $\mathbf{t}$. The rest of the game is same as Game 3. Thus, the two games are statistically indistinguishable.

Game 5: Game 4 has $\mathbf{v} = \mathbf{V} \cdot \mathbf{t} + \mathbf{e}_1 \bmod q$. In this game the challenger C makes $\mathbf{v}$ truly uniform by sampling $\mathbf{y} \overset{\$}{\leftarrow} \mathbb{Z}_q^m$ and setting $\mathbf{v} = \mathbf{y}$. Thus, C makes revocation token totally independent of the bit b. In Game 4, $(\mathbf{V}, \mathbf{v})$ pair is a proper $LWE_{n,q,\chi}$ instance. Thus, the distribution of the pair $(\mathbf{V}, \mathbf{v})$ is computationally close to the uniform distribution over $\mathbb{Z}_q^{m \times n} \times \mathbb{Z}_q^m$. Game 4 and Game 5 are indistinguishable under the assumption of the hardness of $LWE_{n,q,\chi}$ problem. If the adversary can distinguish $\mathbf{v}$ and $\mathbf{y}$, then he can solve Decision-LWE problem.

Game 6: In this game the challenger C modifies the generation of ciphertext $\mathbf{c}_{\mathbf{z}_i} = (\mathbf{c}_1^*, \mathbf{c}_2^*)$ in the challenge phase. Let $\mathbf{c}_1^* = \mathbf{z}_1$ and $\mathbf{c}_2^* = \mathbf{z}_2 + \lfloor q/2 \rfloor d_b$, where $\mathbf{z}_1 \in \mathbb{Z}^m$ and $\mathbf{z}_2 \in \mathbb{Z}^{2m}$ are uniformly random and d_b is the index of the adversary's challenging bit. The rest of the game is same as Game 5. Game 5 and Game 6 are indistinguishable under the assumption of the hardness of $LWE_{n,q,\chi}$. Indeed, if A can distinguish two games, then he can also solve Decision-LWE problem. That means, he can distinguish $(\mathbf{B}^*, (\mathbf{B}^*)^T \mathbf{e}_0 + \mathbf{e}_1)$ from $(\mathbf{B}^*, \mathbf{z}_1)$ and $(\mathbf{G}^*, (\mathbf{G}^*)^T \mathbf{e}_0 + \mathbf{e}_2)$ from $(\mathbf{G}^*, \mathbf{z}_2)$ which conflicts with $LWE_{n,q,\chi}$ assumption.

Game 7: Finally, the challenger C makes Σ^* totally independent of the bit b. C samples $\mathbf{z}_1' \in \mathbb{Z}_q^m$ and $\mathbf{z}_2' \in \mathbb{Z}_q^{2m}$ uniformly random and assigns $\mathbf{c}_1^* = \mathbf{z}_1'$ and $\mathbf{c}_2^* = \mathbf{z}_2'$. Thus, Game 6 and Game 7 are statistically indistinguishable. Since

Game 7 is totally independent from the challenger's bit b, the advantage of the adversary in this game is zero.

Hence, these games prove that our scheme is secure with dynamical-almost-full anonymity, which applied for fully dynamicity.

5.3   Traceability

Theorem 2. *Based on the hardness of* SIS *problem, the proposed scheme is traceable, in the random oracle model.*

Let B be a PPT algorithm that solves SIS problem with non-negligible probability. The adversary A, who has **gpk** and **ok** outputs (M, Σ) in the traceability game. He can add new users and replace members' personal public keys. Moreover, he can query for secret signing keys and revocation tokens of any member. For the queries of A, B answers as in [21] and [20]. In [20], first B selects $coins \leftarrow U(\{0,1,2\})$ as a guess for the misidentification attacks that A will mount. The case $coin = 0$ corresponds, when the knowledge extractor of the proof system reveals witnesses after repeated executions of A and witnesses containing a new identifier $id^* \in \{0,1\}^\ell$ that does not belong to any user. The case $coin = 1$ corresponds to when B expects that the knowledge extractor will obtain the identifier $id^* = id^\dagger$ of a group member in the group. The case $coin = 2$ corresponds to when B is expecting decrypting $\mathbf{c}_{\mathbf{z}_i}^*$ and knowledge extractor will disclose vectors $\mathrm{bin}(\mathbf{z}^*)$, $\mathbf{w}$, and $\mathbf{s}$. Depending on $coin \in \{0,1,2\}$, the group public key is generated using different methods and methods of answering to the queries of A also different as per $coin$.

Finally, A outputs a forgery signature $\Sigma^* = (\mathbf{ovk}^*, \mathbf{c}_{\mathbf{z}_i}^*, \Pi^*, sig^*, \mathbf{v}^*, \rho^*)$ on message M^*. B opens Σ^* and obtains the index. As same as in [21] and [20], the improved Forking Lemma [11] guarantees that, with probability at least $1/2$, B can obtain 3-fork involving tuple $(M, \{CMT^{(k)}\}_{k=1}^t, \mathbf{c}_1, \mathbf{c}_2)$ running A up to $32 \cdot Q_H/(\varepsilon - 3^{-t})$ times with the same tape. Rest of the proof flows as in [20] and finally we can say, if A has non-negligible success probability and runs in polynomial time, then so does B. This concludes our proof of traceability.

5.4   Non-frameability

Theorem 3. *Based on the hardness of* SIS *problem, the proposed scheme is non-frameable, in the random oracle model.*

Suppose there is a frameable adversary A with advantage ϵ, who creates a forgery (M^*, Σ^*) that opens to an innocent, active, and honest user i (i did not sign M^*). We construct a **PPT** algorithm B that solves $SIS_{4n,4m,q,\beta''}$ problem by taking $\bar{A} \in \mathbb{Z}_q^{4n \times 4m}$ and finds a non-zero short vector $\mathbf{w} \in \Lambda_q^\perp(\bar{A})$.

B generates all the public keys and authorities' keys honestly. Then B interacts with A by sending group public key and authority keys. B responses to A's all queries. A can act as a corrupted group manager and add a new user i to the group. When A requests user i to generate a signature on a message M, B generates and returns the signature $\Sigma = (\mathbf{ovk}, \mathbf{c}_{\mathbf{z}_i}, \Pi, sig, \mathbf{v}, \rho)$.

Finally, A outputs $\Sigma^* = (\mathbf{ovk}^*, \mathbf{c}_{\mathbf{z}_i}^*, \Pi^*, sig^*, \mathbf{v}^*, \rho^*)$ signed on a message M^* and which opens to i^* who did not sign the message. Thus, (M^*, Σ^*) should frame user i^*. B has a short vector $\mathbf{z}_{i^*} = \mathbf{F} \cdot \mathbf{x}_{i^*} \bmod q$. To solve SIS instance B should have another short vector $\mathbf{z}_{i'} = \mathbf{F} \cdot \mathbf{x}_{i'} \bmod q$. To compute such a vector, B proceeds by replaying A sufficient times and applying Improved Forking Lemma [11]. As discussed in [20], from the corresponding responses of Π^*, B can extract a short vector $\mathbf{x}\prime$, where $\mathbf{z}_{i^*} = \mathbf{F} \cdot \mathbf{x}\prime \bmod q$. According to the Stern-like proof of knowledge, with overwhelming probability, we say $\mathbf{x}\prime \neq \mathbf{x}_{i^*}$.

This proves the non-frameability of proposed scheme.

6 Conclusion

This paper showed how to obtain member revocation with VLR to the existing member registration scheme [20]. We provided a revocation token generation method that uses a current attribute of the existing scheme. Moreover, we proved the security of the new scheme with the dynamical-almost-full anonymity. For the underlying interactive protocol, we used the protocol given in [20] with the proof of the signer's revocation token which is committed via an LWE function.

Acknowledgments. This work is supported in part by JSPS Grant-in-Aids for Scientic Research (A) JP16H01705 and for Scientic Research (B) JP17H01695.

References

1. Agrawal, S., Boneh, D., Boyen, X.: Efficient lattice (H)IBE in the standard model. In: Gilbert, H. (ed.) EUROCRYPT 2010. LNCS, vol. 6110, pp. 553–572. Springer, Heidelberg (2010). https://doi.org/10.1007/978-3-642-13190-5_28
2. Alwen, J., Peikert, C.: Generating shorter bases for hard random lattices. In: STACS 2009, pp. 75–86 (2009)
3. Ateniese, G., Song, D., Tsudik, G.: Quasi-efficient revocation of group signatures. In: Blaze, M. (ed.) FC 2002. LNCS, vol. 2357, pp. 183–197. Springer, Heidelberg (2003). https://doi.org/10.1007/3-540-36504-4_14
4. Bellare, M., Micciancio, D., Warinschi, B.: Foundations of group signatures: formal definitions, simplified requirements, and a construction based on general assumptions. In: Biham, E. (ed.) EUROCRYPT 2003. LNCS, vol. 2656, pp. 614–629. Springer, Heidelberg (2003). https://doi.org/10.1007/3-540-39200-9_38
5. Bellare, M., Shi, H., Zhang, C.: Foundations of group signatures: the case of dynamic groups. In: Menezes, A. (ed.) CT-RSA 2005. LNCS, vol. 3376, pp. 136–153. Springer, Heidelberg (2005). https://doi.org/10.1007/978-3-540-30574-3_11
6. Boneh, D., Boyen, X., Shacham, H.: Short group signatures. In: Franklin, M. (ed.) CRYPTO 2004. LNCS, vol. 3152, pp. 41–55. Springer, Heidelberg (2004). https://doi.org/10.1007/978-3-540-28628-8_3
7. Boneh, D., Shacham, H.: Group signatures with verifier-local revocation. In: ACM-CCS 2004, pp. 168–177. ACM (2004)
8. Bootle, J., Cerulli, A., Chaidos, P., Ghadafi, E., Groth, J.: Foundations of fully dynamic group signatures. In: Manulis, M., Sadeghi, A.-R., Schneider, S. (eds.) ACNS 2016. LNCS, vol. 9696, pp. 117–136. Springer, Cham (2016). https://doi.org/10.1007/978-3-319-39555-5_7

9. Brakerski, Z., Langlois, A., Peikert, C., Regev, O., Stehlé, D.: Classical hardness of learning with errors. In: STOC 2013, pp. 575–584. ACM (2013)
10. Brickell, E.: An efficient protocol for anonymously providing assurance of the container of the private key. Submitted to the Trusted Computing Group, April 2003
11. Brickell, E., Pointcheval, D., Vaudenay, S., Yung, M.: Design validations for discrete logarithm based signature schemes. In: Imai, H., Zheng, Y. (eds.) PKC 2000. LNCS, vol. 1751, pp. 276–292. Springer, Heidelberg (2000). https://doi.org/10.1007/978-3-540-46588-1_19
12. Camenisch, J., Lysyanskaya, A.: Dynamic accumulators and application to efficient revocation of anonymous credentials. In: Yung, M. (ed.) CRYPTO 2002. LNCS, vol. 2442, pp. 61–76. Springer, Heidelberg (2002). https://doi.org/10.1007/3-540-45708-9_5
13. Camenisch, J., Neven, G., Rückert, M.: Fully anonymous attribute tokens from lattices. In: Visconti, I., De Prisco, R. (eds.) SCN 2012. LNCS, vol. 7485, pp. 57–75. Springer, Heidelberg (2012). https://doi.org/10.1007/978-3-642-32928-9_4
14. Chaum, D., van Heyst, E.: Group signatures. In: Davies, D.W. (ed.) EUROCRYPT 1991. LNCS, vol. 547, pp. 257–265. Springer, Heidelberg (1991). https://doi.org/10.1007/3-540-46416-6_22
15. Gentry, C., Peikert, C., Vaikuntanathan, V.: Trapdoors for hard lattices and new cryptographic constructions. In: ACM 2008, pp. 197–206. ACM (2008)
16. Gordon, S.D., Katz, J., Vaikuntanathan, V.: A group signature scheme from lattice assumptions. In: Abe, M. (ed.) ASIACRYPT 2010. LNCS, vol. 6477, pp. 395–412. Springer, Heidelberg (2010). https://doi.org/10.1007/978-3-642-17373-8_23
17. Kawachi, A., Tanaka, K., Xagawa, K.: Concurrently secure identification schemes based on the worst-case hardness of lattice problems. In: Pieprzyk, J. (ed.) ASIACRYPT 2008. LNCS, vol. 5350, pp. 372–389. Springer, Heidelberg (2008). https://doi.org/10.1007/978-3-540-89255-7_23
18. Kiayias, A., Yung, M.: Secure scalable group signature with dynamic joins and separable authorities. Int. J. Secur. Netw. 1(1–2), 24–45 (2006)
19. Langlois, A., Ling, S., Nguyen, K., Wang, H.: Lattice-based group signature scheme with verifier-local revocation. In: Krawczyk, H. (ed.) PKC 2014. LNCS, vol. 8383, pp. 345–361. Springer, Heidelberg (2014). https://doi.org/10.1007/978-3-642-54631-0_20
20. Libert, B., Ling, S., Mouhartem, F., Nguyen, K., Wang, H.: Signature schemes with efficient protocols and dynamic group signatures from lattice assumptions. In: Cheon, J.H., Takagi, T. (eds.) ASIACRYPT 2016. LNCS, vol. 10032, pp. 373–403. Springer, Heidelberg (2016). https://doi.org/10.1007/978-3-662-53890-6_13
21. Ling, S., Nguyen, K., Wang, H.: Group signatures from lattices: simpler, tighter, shorter, ring-based. In: Katz, J. (ed.) PKC 2015. LNCS, vol. 9020, pp. 427–449. Springer, Heidelberg (2015). https://doi.org/10.1007/978-3-662-46447-2_19
22. Ling, S., Nguyen, K., Wang, H., Xu, Y.: Lattice-based group signatures: achieving full dynamicity with ease. In: Gollmann, D., Miyaji, A., Kikuchi, H. (eds.) ACNS 2017. LNCS, vol. 10355, pp. 293–312. Springer, Cham (2017). https://doi.org/10.1007/978-3-319-61204-1_15
23. Peikert, C.: A decade of lattice cryptography. Found. Trends Theor. Comput. Sci. 10(4), 283–424 (2016). https://doi.org/10.1561/0400000074
24. Perera, M.N.S., Koshiba, T.: Achieving almost-full security for lattice-based fully dynamic group signatures with verifier-local revocation. In: ISPEC 2018. LNCS (2018, to appear)

25. Perera, M.N.S., Koshiba, T.: Fully dynamic group signature scheme with member registration and verifier-local revocation. In: ICMC 2018. Mathematics and Computing (2018, to appear)
26. Perera, M.N.S., Koshiba, T.: Zero-knowledge proof for lattice-based group signature schemes with verifier-local revocation. In: 9th International Workshop on Trustworthy Computing and Security (TwCSec-2018). LNDT (2018, to appear)
27. Regev, O.: On lattices, learning with errors, random linear codes, and cryptography. In: STOC 2005, pp. 84–93. ACM Press (2005)

Modular Verification of Sequential Composition for Private Channels in Maude-NPA

Fan Yang[1(✉)], Santiago Escobar[2], Catherine Meadows[3(✉)], and José Meseguer[1]

[1] University of Illinois at Urbana-Champaign, Champaign, IL, USA
{fanyang6,meseguer}@illinois.edu
[2] Universitat Politècnica de València, Valencia, Spain
sescobar@dsic.upv.es
[3] Naval Research Laboratory, Washington, DC, USA
meadows@itd.nrl.navy.mil

Abstract. This paper gives a *modular verification* methodology in which, given parametric specifications of a key establishment protocol P and a protocol Q providing private channel communication, security and authenticity properties of their sequential composition $P \; ; \; Q$ can be reduced to: (i) verification of corresponding properties for P, and (ii) verification of corresponding properties for an *abstract version* Q^α of Q in which keys have been suitably abstracted. Our results improve upon previous work in this area in several ways. First of all, we both support a large class of equational theories and provide tool support via the Maude-NPA cryptographic protocol analysis tool. Secondly as long as certain conditions on P and Q guaranteeing the secrecy of keys inherited by Q from P are satisfied, our results apply to the composition of any two reachability properties of the two protocols.

1 Introduction

Security protocols often depend on other protocols to generate the keys and other values they use to communicate securely. This can often be modeled in terms of protocol composition: the protocol receiving the keys runs as a subroutine of the protocol that generates the keys. But examining composed protocols can be unwieldy, leading to state space explosion.

Researchers have developed two primary ways of approaching this problem. One is to think of the parent protocol as creating *secure channels* that the child protocol can use for secure communication. Another approach is to perform modular verification, in which the two protocols are analyzed separately, and conclusions about the composition are made based on the results.

Partially supported by the EU (FEDER) and the Spanish MINECO under grant TIN 2015-69175-C4-1-R, by the Generalitat Valenciana under grant PROMETEOII/2015/013, by the US Air Force Office of Scientific Research under award number FA9550-17-1-0286, and by NRL under contract number N00173-17-1-G002.

S. K. Katsikas and C. Alcaraz (Eds.): STM 2018, LNCS 11091, pp. 20–36, 2018.
https://doi.org/10.1007/978-3-030-01141-3_2

Secure channels and modular verification are closely related, and indeed we can think of them as two different kinds of decomposition, the main difference being that the channels specified in one approach are left implicit in the other. However, they have usually been treated separately. But the close relationship raises the possibility that techniques developed for one can be used for another.

In this paper we take advantage of this relationship to make use of a construct used by Cheval, Cortier, and Le Morvan [3] to reason about secure channels to prove results about modular decomposition. This construct is called an *encapsulation*. It is a combination of different cryptographic operators that is used to provide such functionality as confidentiality and authentication. But its usefulness to modular composition lies in the fact that it is impossible for encapsulations to leak the keys used to construct them, so that any leakage that occurs must be the fault of the protocol providing the keys. We can thus think of an encapsulation together with the keys used to implement it as providing a secure communication channel, although unlike [3] we do not define the properties of the channels explicitly; rather they are verified implicitly by the separate analyses of the child protocols.

Example 1. We use the Passive Authentication (PA) protocol [3] as a running example, which provides an authentication mechanism proving that the content of the RFID chip in an E-passport is authentic. We describe below the PA protocol, between a passport (P) and a reader (R). A secure channel between principals A and B is represented as an encapsulation expression $\mathcal{E}(M, \overrightarrow{K})$ where M is the payload message and $\overrightarrow{K}$ is a list of keys.

$$R \rightarrow P : \mathcal{E}(read, \overrightarrow{K})$$
$$P \rightarrow R : \mathcal{E}(data; sign(h(data), sk(P)), \overrightarrow{K})$$

In this protocol, $data$ is the passport information, h is a hash function, $sign(M, K)$ is signing message M with key K, and $sk(P)$ is the signing key of P.

A protocol using channels is parametric in several ways: (i) how is the encapsulation $\mathcal{E}$ actually obtained using cryptographic primitives, and (ii) what keys $\overrightarrow{K}$ are actually needed by such encapsulation. In [3], the encapsulation associated to protocol PA is achieved by using symmetric encryption and MAC with two respective keys: $\mathcal{E}(M, K_1, K_2) = senc(M, K_1); mac(senc(M, K_1), K_2)$.

To obtain the actual keys, we first run a key establishment protocol that is sequentially composed with PA. The cryptographic protocol analysis tool Maude-NPA [9] was extended in [15] with a specification language, a semantics, and automatic verification methods that support sequential protocol composition.

Example 2. The Basic Access Control (BAC) protocol [3] for access control on private data is used as the key establishment protocol for the PA protocol.

$$R \to P : challenge$$
$$P \to R : Np$$
$$R \to P : senc(Nr; Np; Kr, Ke), mac(senc(Nr; Np; Kr, Ke), Km)$$
$$P \to R : senc(Np; Nr; Kp, Ke), mac(senc(Np; Nr; Kp, Ke), Km)$$

The sequential protocol composition BAC ; PA is then achieved running one protocol after the other and passing information from BAC to PA, see Sect. 2.

Our Contributions. The main contribution of this paper is a *modular verification* methodology in which, given parametric specifications of a key establishment protocol P and a protocol Q providing private channel communication, security and authenticity properties of their sequential composition P ; Q can be reduced to: (i) verification of corresponding properties for P, and (ii) verification of corresponding properties for an *abstract version* Q^α of Q in which keys have been suitably abstracted. The semantic basis of this methodology is provided by two *simulation relations* H_P and H_Q of the form $P \xleftarrow{H_P} P$; $Q \xrightarrow{H_Q} Q^\alpha$ that essentially "project out" states of P ; Q to, respectively, states of P and states of Q^α. This then ensures that given an attack state for P ; Q, if no attack of types (i), resp. (ii), exists for P, resp. Q, no such attack of the specified kind exists for P ; Q. In addition we offer tool support via the Maude-NPA cryptographic protocol analysis tool [9]. Furthermore, we are able to easily handle algebraic properties of P, Q, and the encapsulation $\mathcal{E}$, (e.g. Diffie-Hellman exponentiation used in the IKEv1 protocol; see Sect. 6) as long as they satisfy the *finite variant property*, which is also supported by Maude-NPA.

Plan of the Paper. The rest of this paper is organized as follows. In Sect. 2 we give a description of Maude-NPA, including its strand model, notation and semantics for protocol composition and its rewriting based forwards semantics. In Section 3 we present an approach to model channels with security assumptions in Maude-NPA. In Sect. 4 we present a modular method for reducing reachability properties of $P;Q$ to corresponding such properties for P and Q's abstraction Q^α. In Sect. 5 we explain how this modular methodology is supported by Maude-NPA. In Sect. 6 we present some example protocols we analyzed using our modular approach.

2   Maude-NPA

In Maude-NPA, as in most formal analysis tools for cryptographic protocols, a protocol is modeled as a set of rules. Specifically, as a rewrite theory $\mathcal{P}$ that describes the actions of honest principals communicating across a network controlled by an intruder. Given a protocol $\mathcal{P} = (\Sigma_\mathcal{P}, E_\mathcal{P}, R_\mathcal{P})$, states in Maude-NPA are modeled as elements of an initial algebra $\mathcal{T}_{\Sigma_\mathcal{P}/E_\mathcal{P}}$, where

$\Sigma_{\mathcal{P}} = \Sigma_{SS} \cup \Sigma_{\mathcal{C}}$ is the signature defining the sorts and function symbols ($\Sigma_{\mathcal{C}}$ for the cryptographic functions and Σ_{SS} for all the state constructor symbols), $E_{\mathcal{P}} = E_{\mathcal{C}} \cup E_{SS}$ is a set of equations where $E_{\mathcal{C}}$ specifies the *algebraic properties* of the cryptographic functions and E_{SS} denotes properties of constructors of states, and $R_{\mathcal{P}}$ are the protocol and intruder transition rules. The set of equations $E_{\mathcal{C}}$ may vary depending on different protocols, but the set of equations E_{SS} is always the same for all protocols. Therefore, a state is an $E_{\mathcal{P}}$-equivalence class $[t]_{E_{\mathcal{P}}} \in T_{\Sigma_{\mathcal{P}}/E_{\mathcal{P}}}$ with t a ground $\Sigma_{\mathcal{P}}$-term, i.e., a term without variables.

In Maude-NPA a *state* is a term $t \in T_{\Sigma_{\mathcal{P}}/E_{\mathcal{P}}}$ of sort State which has the form $\{S_1 \,\&\, \cdots \,\&\, S_n \,\&\, \{IK\}\}$, where $\&$ is an infix associative-commutative union operator with identity symbol $\emptyset$. Each element in the set is either a *strand* S_i or the *intruder knowledge* $\{IK\}$ at that state.

The *intruder knowledge* $\{IK\}$ belongs to the state and is represented as a set of facts using comma as an infix associative-commutative union operator with identity element *empty*. There are two kinds of intruder facts: *positive* knowledge facts (the intruder knows m, i.e., $m \in \mathcal{I}$), and *negative* knowledge facts (the intruder *does not yet know* m but *will know it in a future state*, i.e., $m \notin \mathcal{I}$), where m is a message expression.

A *strand* [10] specifies the sequence of messages sent and received by a principal executing the protocol and is represented as a sequence of messages $[msg_1^{\pm}, msg_2^{\pm}, msg_3^{\pm}, \dots, msg_{k-1}^{\pm}, msg_k^{\pm}]$ with $msg_i^{\pm}$ either msg_i^{-} (also written $-msg_i$) representing an input message, or msg_i^{+} (also written $+msg_i$) representing an output message. Note that each msg_i is a term of a special sort Msg. Variables of a special sort Fresh are used to represent pseudo-random values (nonces) and Maude-NPA ensures that two distinct fresh variables will never be merged. Strands are prefixed with all the fresh variables $f_1, \dots, f_k$ created by that strand, i.e., $:: f_1, \dots, f_k :: [msg_1^{\pm}, msg_2^{\pm}, \dots, msg_k^{\pm}]$.

Strands are used to represent both the actions of honest principals (with a strand specified for each protocol role) and the actions of an intruder (with a strand for each action an intruder is able to perform on messages). In Maude-NPA strands evolve over time; the symbol $|$ is used to divide past and future. That is, given a strand $[\, msg_1^{\pm}, \ \dots, \ msg_i^{\pm} \mid msg_{i+1}^{\pm}, \ \dots, \ msg_k^{\pm} \,]$, messages $msg_1^{\pm}, \dots, msg_i^{\pm}$ are the *past messages*, and messages $msg_{i+1}^{\pm}, \dots, msg_k^{\pm}$ are the *future messages* ($msg_{i+1}^{\pm}$ is the immediate future message). A strand $[msg_1^{\pm}, \dots, msg_k^{\pm}]$ is shorthand for $[nil \mid msg_1^{\pm}, \dots, msg_k^{\pm}, nil]$. An *initial state* is a state where the bar is at the beginning for all strands in the state, and the intruder knowledge has no fact of the form $m \in \mathcal{I}$. A *final state* is a state where the bar is at the end for all strands in the state and there is no intruder fact of the form $m \notin \mathcal{I}$.

Since the number of states in $T_{\Sigma_{\mathcal{P}}/E_{\mathcal{P}}}$ is in general infinite, rather than exploring concrete protocol states $[t]_{E_{\mathcal{P}}} \in T_{\Sigma_{\mathcal{P}}/E_{\mathcal{P}}}$, Maude-NPA explores *symbolic state patterns* $[t(x_1, \dots, x_n)]_{E_{\mathcal{P}}} \in T_{\Sigma_{\mathcal{P}}/E_{\mathcal{P}}}(\mathcal{X})$ on the free $(\Sigma_{\mathcal{P}}, E_{\mathcal{P}})$-algebra over a set of variables $\mathcal{X}$. In this way, a state pattern $[t(x_1, \dots, x_n)]_{E_{\mathcal{P}}}$ represents not a single concrete state (i.e., an $E_{\mathcal{P}}$-equivalence class) but a possibly infinite set of states (i.e., an infinite set of $E_{\mathcal{P}}$-equivalence classes), namely all the *instances* of the pattern $[t(x_1, \ldots, x_n)]_{E_{\mathcal{P}}}$ where the variables $x_1, \ldots, x_n$ have been instantiated by concrete ground terms.

The forwards semantics of Maude-NPA [9] is expressed in terms of *rewrite rules* $R_{\mathcal{P}}$ that describe how a protocol transitions from one state to another via the intruder's interaction with it. The rewrite rules are automatically extracted from the strand specification $SS_{\mathcal{P}}$ of a protocol. Maude-NPA can find an attack by specifying an insecure state pattern called an *attack pattern*.

To support sequential protocol composition, strands can be extended with *synchronization messages* [15] of the form $\{Role_1 \rightarrow Role_2 \ ;; \ mode \ ;; \ w\}$ where $Role_1, Role_2$ are constants of sort Role provided by the user, $mode$ can be either 1-1 or 1-* representing a one-to-one or one-to-many synchronization (whether an output message can synchronize with one or many input messages), and w is a term representing the information passed along in the synchronization messages.

Example 3. The PA protocol of Example 1 is specified in Maude-NPA by two strands associated to the reader (R) and passport (P) roles. To be composable with a previous key establishment protocol, these strands have *input parameters* (inside a synchronization message's curly braces). The passport strand is:

$$(P) :: r' :: [nil \mid \{Prev2 \rightarrow PA.P \ ;; \ 1\text{--}1 \ ;; \ R; P; K_1; K_2\}, -(\mathcal{E}(read, K_1, K_2)),$$
$$+(\mathcal{E}(data(P, r'); sign(h(data(P, r')), sk(P)), K_1, K_2)), nil]$$

Example 4. The BAC protocol of Example 2 is specified in Maude-NPA by two strands associated to the reader (R) and passport (P) roles. To be usable for sequential composition with another protocol, these strands have *output parameters* (inside a synchronization message's curly braces). The passport strand is:

$$(P) :: r, r_2 :: [nil \mid -(challenge), \ +(n(P, r)), -(senc(N_R; n(P, r); K_R, ke(P, R));$$
$$mac(senc(N_R; n(P, r); K_R, ke(P, R)), km(P, R))), +(senc(n(P, r); N_R; key(P, r_2),$$
$$ke(P, R)); mac(senc(n(P, r); N_R; key(P, r_2), ke(P, R)), km(P, R))),$$
$$\{BAC.P \rightarrow PA.P \ ;; \ 1\text{--}1 \ ;; \ R; P; f_1(K_R, key(P, r_2)); f_2(K_R, key(P, r_2))\}, nil]$$

Example 5. Given the protocol specification of PA in Example 3 and of *BAC* in Example 4, a concrete state where a strand of the passport role in BAC has been synchronized with a strand of the passport role in PA looks as follows:

$$(BAC.P)$$
$$[\ldots, \{BAC.P \rightarrow PA.P; ; 1\text{--}1; ; R; P; f_1(K_R, key(P, r_2)); f_2(K_R, key(P, r_2))\} \mid nil] \ \&$$
$$(PA.P) \ [\{BAC.P \rightarrow PA.P; ; 1\text{--}1; ; R; P; f_1(K_R, key(P, r_2)); f_2(K_R, key(P, r_2))\} \mid \ldots]$$

3   Protocol Specification with Encapsulations

To specify and analyze protocols using encapsulations in Maude-NPA, in this section we add special sorts and operations to the Maude-NPA message notation that we introduced in Sect. 2. Messages sent and received through encapsulations are denoted by terms constructed using these special sorts and operations.

A protocol Q providing private communication is such that all input and output messages in a strand are actually sent through (possibly different) encapsulations. Its specification has the form $Q = (\Sigma_Q, E_Q, R_Q)$, where the signature Σ_Q is a disjoint union of $\Sigma_{Ch} \uplus \Sigma_{Q_0}$ and where:

1. Σ_{Ch} is the signature of *encapsulation operators* used in the private channels, which have the general form: $\mathcal{E} : \mathsf{QMsg} \times \mathsf{QKey} \times \cdots \times \mathsf{QKey} \to \mathcal{E}\mathsf{Msg}$ where QMsg denotes the sort of *payload messages* sent through the encapsulation, QKey denotes the sort of *keys* used in the encapsulation, and $\mathcal{E}\mathsf{Msg}$ is the sort of *encapsulated messages*, representing message transmission. There is also a general sort Msg of Maude-NPA for messages, and subsort inclusions $\mathsf{QMsg} < \mathcal{E}\mathsf{Msg} < \mathsf{Msg}$ and $\mathsf{QKey} < \mathsf{Msg}$.
2. Σ_{Q_0} is the signature of *cryptographic functions* used to *actually achieve the encapsulation*, i.e., to give concrete meaning to the operator $\mathcal{E}$ in Σ_{Ch}. All operators in Σ_{Q_0} are of the general form $f : \mathsf{S}_1 \times \cdots \times \mathsf{S}_n \to \mathcal{E}\mathsf{Msg}$, where $\{\mathsf{S}_1, \ldots, \mathsf{S}_n\} \subseteq \{\mathsf{QKey}, \mathcal{E}\mathsf{Msg}\}$.
3. E_Q is also a disjoint union $E_Q = E_\mathcal{E} \uplus E_{Q_0} \uplus B_{Q_0}$ where $E_\mathcal{E}$ are the *definitional extensions* of the operators $\mathcal{E}$ in Σ_{Ch} in terms of those in Σ_Q having the form: $\mathcal{E}(M, X_1, \ldots, X_n) = t(M, X_1, \ldots, X_n)$ with $t(M, X_1, \ldots, X_n)$ being a Σ_{Q_0}-term of sort $\mathcal{E}\mathsf{Msg}$. B_{Q_0} is a set of Σ_{Q_0}-axioms and E_{Q_0} are Σ_0-equations that are convergent (confluent and terminating) modulo B_{Q_0}.

The encapsulation equations $E_\mathcal{E}$ define how cryptographic primitives are used to implement private communication. We assume that a protocol Q is specified using protocol composition to define how the extra parameters of an encapsulation (principal identifiers and keys) are bound.

Example 6. Given Example 3, the encapsulation symbol $\mathcal{E} : \mathsf{QMsg} \times \mathsf{QKey} \times \mathsf{QKey} \to \mathcal{E}\mathsf{Msg}$ for a secure communication is defined as $\mathcal{E}(M, K_1, K_2) = senc(M, K_1); mac(senc(M, K_1), K_2)$. The two keys K_1 and K_2 are generated by a key establishment protocol for the passport (P) and the reader (R).

We assume the following *admissibility requirements* on the *definitional extensions* equations $E_\mathcal{E}$ of the encapsulation operators $\mathcal{E}$:

- certain positions in the term $t_\mathcal{E}$ associated by $E_\mathcal{E}$ to the encapsulation operator $\mathcal{E}$ are designated as *non-payload* positions and are not of sort QMsg;
- it is impossible for the intruder to learn a term that only appears in non-payload positions in such a term $t_\mathcal{E}$, and
- since QKey is not a subsort of QMsg, expressions of sort QKey only appear in non-payload positions in $t_\mathcal{E}$.

For example, in $senc(M, K_1); mac(senc(M, K_1), K_2)$, the non-payload positions are 1.2, 2.1.2, and 2.2, i.e., the positions where K_1 and K_2 occur.

Given a protocol Q, from the actual protocol composition P ; Q with a key establishment protocol P it is possible to derive a *key implementation map* ρ^P that defines the correspondence between an encapsulation $\mathcal{E}$ and a list of keys established by the protocol P. Indeed, we will denote a protocol composition as $P ;_\rho Q$ to emphasize the specific key map ρ. The keys are assigned considering not only the type of desired communication, but also the names and roles of the sender and the receiver of each protocol. More specifically, a key implementation map takes two arguments: the first argument is a triple denoting the sender's name, sender's role in protocol P and sender's role in protocol Q; the second argument is a triple denoting the receiver's name, receiver's role in protocol P and receiver's role in protocol Q.

Example 7. Following Example 2, the key implementation map is:

$$\rho^{BAC.P}((P, BAC.P, PA.P), (R, BAC.R, PA.R))$$
$$= \{K_{1P,R}^{PA.P} \mapsto f_1(K_R, key(P, r_2)), K_{2P,R}^{PA.P} \mapsto f_2(K_R, key(P, r_2))\},$$
$$\rho^{BAC.R}((P, BAC.P, PA.P), (R, BAC.R, PA.R))$$
$$= \{K_{1P,R}^{PA.R} \mapsto f_1(key(R, r_1), K_P), K_{2P,R}^{PA.R} \mapsto f_2(key(R, r_1), K_P)\}$$

Although the keys in $\rho^{BAC.P}$ and $\rho^{BAC.R}$ are syntactically different, the keys can be unified, which captures the idea that different roles may have different views of the same message.

We assume the following *admissibility requirements* on ρ:

- **Q keys are actual P keys of sort QKey.** For any $\rho^{Rol_P}(\widehat{A}, \widehat{B}) = \{\overrightarrow{X}_{A,B}^{Rol_Q} \mapsto \overrightarrow{K}\}$, $Var(\overrightarrow{K}) \subseteq Var(\mathcal{P}_P|_{Rol_P})$, where $\overrightarrow{K}$ denotes a list of QKeys.
- **Keys must include some random value of sort Fresh.** For any $\rho^{Rol_P}(\widehat{A}, \widehat{B}) = \{\overrightarrow{X}_{A,B}^{Rol_Q} \mapsto \overrightarrow{K}\}, \forall K_i \in \overrightarrow{K}$, there exists r:Fresh s.t. $r \in Var(K_i)$.
- **Keys are disjoint.** No two keys bound by ρ^{Rol_P} are unifiable.
- **ρ is injective, even after substitution.** For $\rho^{Rol_P}(\widehat{A}, \widehat{B}) = \{\overrightarrow{X}_{A,B}^{Rol_Q} \mapsto \overrightarrow{K}\}$ and $\rho^{Rol_P'}(\widehat{A'}, \widehat{B'}) = \{\overrightarrow{X}_{A',B'}^{Rol_Q'} \mapsto \overrightarrow{K'}\}$, we require that there exists a substitution θ such that $(\widehat{A}, \widehat{B})\theta = (\widehat{A'}, \widehat{B'})\theta$, iff there exists σ such that $\overrightarrow{K}\theta\sigma =_{E_P \cup B_P} \overrightarrow{K'}\theta\sigma$ (resp. $(\overrightarrow{K}\theta\sigma)^{-1} =_{E_P \cup B_P} \overrightarrow{K'}\theta\sigma$ for asymmetric keys).

The encapsulation equations $E_\mathcal{E}$ and the above map ρ^P jointly define a translation function: $(\mathcal{E}, \rho^P) : \mathcal{T}_{\Sigma_Q}(X)_{\mathsf{ChMsg}} \to \mathcal{T}_{\Sigma_{\mathsf{QMsg}} \cup \Sigma_{\mathsf{QKey}} \cup \Sigma_{Q_0}}(X)$, which models the actual composition of all the strands involved between the key establishment protocol P and the protocol Q with private communication:

$$\mathcal{E}(M, X_{1A,B}^{Rol_Q}, \ldots, X_{n_{ch_{op}}A,B}^{Rol_Q})\rho_{ch_{op}}^{Rol_P}(\widehat{A}, \widehat{B})$$

We will refer to the child protocol in the composition $P;_\rho Q$ as Q^ρ in the rest of this paper. To simplify the notation, we will use $E_;$ for $E_{P;_\rho Q}$ and $B_;$ for $B_{P;_\rho Q}$. We summarize the *syntactic disjointness assumptions* between P and Q implied by this setup as follows:

- all the messages in honest protocol strands of protocol Q^ρ are encapsulated, i.e., are of sort $\mathcal{E}$Msg, and all messages in protocol P are of a sort PMsg or subsorts of a sort PMsg.

– all the messages that can be shared by protocol P and Q^ρ must be of sorts QKey, a new sort Shared or subsorts of Shared.

Note that QKey is not a subsort of $\mathcal{E}$Msg, therefore the keys generated by protocol P cannot be unified with encapsulations or payload messages in Q^ρ, i.e., messages of sort QMsg. By the disjointness feature of this setup, all information synchronized through input-output parameters in the protocol $P;_\rho Q$ are of sort QKey, Shared or subsort of Shared. This setup is inspired by some of the common assumptions: (i) in the child protocol of $P;_\rho Q$, the keys used to implement encapsulations will never be sent in plain text or as a payload message; (ii) protocols P, Q and encapsulations in $\mathcal{E}$ have disjoint encryption subterms.

4 Behavioral Decomposition of $P;_\rho Q$

In this section we show that the composed protocol $P;_\rho Q$ can be analyzed by analyzing the protocols P and Q^α (an abstraction of Q^ρ) separately.

In the rest of this paper we will use S to denote states, SS to denote the set of strands in a state, and IK to denote the intruder knowledge set in a state. Different subscripts are used to distinguish states, strands and intruder knowledge of different protocols. Given a set of strands SS, we denote by $SS|_Q$ (resp. $SS|_P$) the strands in the strand set SS that are (partial) instances of strands in the protocol Q (resp. P) without input (resp. output) parameters, $SS|_{HS}$ (resp. $SS|_{DY}$) the strands in SS that are instances of honest protocol strands (resp. Dolev-Yao strands).

4.1 Simulation of $P;_\rho Q$ by P

In this section we show that protocol P can simulate protocol $P;_\rho Q$ so that any QKey can be generated by $P;_\rho Q$ if and only if it can be generated by P.

We first define the simulation relation below. Note that we only consider states that are reachable from initial states.

Definition 1 (Relation $\mathcal{H}_P$). *Let $S_; = SS_; \,\&\, IK_;$ denote a state that is reachable from the initial state in protocol $P;_\rho Q$, and $S_P = SS_P \,\&\, IK_P$ denote a state that is reachable from the initial state in protocol P, the relation $\mathcal{H}_P$ between states in $P;_\rho Q$ and in P is defined by the equivalence $(S_;, S_P) \in \mathcal{H}_P$ if and only if:*

(i) $SS_;|_P|_{HS} =_{E_P \cup B_P} SS_P|_{HS}$, and $SS_;|_P|_{DY} \subseteq_{E_P \cup B_P} SS_P|_{DY}$,
(ii) $IK_;|_{\Sigma_P} =_{E_P \cup B_P} IK_P$

We have proved that the relation $\mathcal{H}_P$ defined above is indeed a simulation relation. The following lemma is essential for the main results below.

Lemma 1. *Given terms $t, t' \in T_{\Sigma_{P;_\rho Q}}(X)|_{\Sigma_P}$, $t =_{E_P \cup B_P} t'$ iff $t =_{E_; \cup B_;} t'$.*

Theorem 1 (Soundness from $P;_\rho Q$ to P). *Given a key establishment protocol P, a key application protocol Q, and the composed protocol $P;_\rho Q$, if a state $S;$ is reachable from the initial state of protocol $P;_\rho Q$, then there exists a state S_P that is reachable from the initial state in P and such that $(S;, S_P) \in \mathcal{H}_P$.*

Theorem 2 (Completeness from $P;_\rho Q$ to P). *Given a key establishment protocol P, a key application protocol Q, and the composed protocol $P;_\rho Q$, if a state S is reachable from the initial state in P, the state S is reachable from the initial state of protocol $P;_\rho Q$.*

By Theorems 1 and 2 we can conclude that any authentication or secrecy property of the QKeys holds in P if and only if it holds in $P;_\rho Q$. In particular, this holds for the following property.

Definition 2. *A protocol P is* Secrecy-Enforcing *if any state where an honest principal has accepted a list of QKeys to communicate with another honest principal and the intruder learns any of the secret QKeys is unreachable in P.*

In the rest of this paper, we assume that the key establishment protocol P is *Secrecy-Enforcing*. Note that the intruder can still learn keys from communications in P, either because some the participants of the protocol are compromised or because the keys were not intended to be secret in the first place.

4.2   Simulation of $P;_\rho Q$ by Q^α

In this section we show that the reachability properties of the protocol $P;_\rho Q$ can be simulated by an abstraction of Q^ρ, denoted Q^α, where actual keys from an admissible P are replaced by their abstraction using a mapping α. The inherited keys become in some sense independent of the protocol P.

The key abstraction mapping α can be different for each specific protocol. Usually it is enough to consider the abstraction of the key patterns that can be synchronized from protocol P to protocol Q in any reachable states, as specified by the mapping ρ. Note that the mapping ρ can be optimized to be more precise by running analysis in protocol P. Let $t(x_1, \ldots, x_n)$ denote any such key pattern. We assume all such patterns are *strongly irreducible*, i.e., they, and all their instances by irreducible substitutions are irreducible by equations E_P modulo axioms B_P. Note that in Q the sort QKey is *parametric*: it is instantiated to different data types for keys depending on the choice of P. The central intuition about the abstract protocol Q^α is that the keys that are instances of each key pattern $t(x_1, \ldots, x_n)$ in ρ are abstracted by *constructor terms* using some new constructors Ω, possibly modulo some axioms B_Ω. Furthermore, key terms that cannot unify with any of the key patterns, are mapped to a special constant in Ω, e.g., c. In this way, Q^α terms of sort QKey become *constructor terms* up to B_Ω-equivalence, thus greatly simplifying their representation. Different choices of key abstraction are possible (see Example 8 below for a concrete illustration). Here is the general method:

Definition 3 (Key Abstraction). *A key abstraction α of protocol Q^ρ by protocol Q^α is defined as follows: (i) new key-building constructors Ω and axioms B_Ω are specified, including a special constant c in Ω, (ii) for each key pattern $t(x_1, \ldots, x_n)$ in ρ, a constructor Ω-term $u_t(x_{i_1}, \ldots, x_{i_k})$ with $\{x_{i_1}, \ldots, x_{i_k}\} \subseteq \{x_1, \ldots, x_n\}$ is chosen, and (iii) the key abstraction α is defined by equations $\alpha(t(x_1, \ldots, x_n)) = u_t(x_{i_1}, \ldots, x_{i_k})$ for each key pattern $t(x_1, \ldots, x_n)$ in ρ, plus an additional "otherwise" default equation "$\alpha(t) = c$ [otherwise]" (that applies to any t that does not $E_P \cup B_P$-unify with any of the key patterns) subject to the requirements: (1) For each key pattern $t(x_1, \ldots, x_n)$ in ρ,*

$$t(x_1, \ldots, x_n) =_{E_P \cup B_P} t(x'_1, \ldots, x'_n) \;\Rightarrow\; u_t(x_{i_1}, \ldots, x_{i_k}) =_{B_\Omega} u_t(x'_{i_1}, \ldots, x'_{i_k})$$

which ensures that α maps $E_P \cup B_P$-equivalence classes of keys in Q^ρ to B_Ω-equivalence classes of keys in Q^α. (2) The abstract key implementation map for Q^α obtained by composing ρ with α satisfies the same admissibility requirements as the original map ρ (see Sect. 3).

Example 8. An example key abstraction α for a reader and a passport's keys in a concrete reachable state of the protocol PA^ρ according to the key mapping is:

$$\alpha(f_1(key(reader, r_1), key(passport, r_2))) = k_1(reader, passport, r_1),$$
$$\alpha(f_2(key(reader, r_1), key(passport, r_2))) = k_2(reader, passport, r_2),$$

where $\Omega = \{k_1, k_2, c\}$ and $B_\Omega = \emptyset$. This α satisfies the admissibility requirements since it ensures that every key is abstracted differently by using the participants of BAC and a fresh variable that is involved in the key.

Note that the protocol Q^α also extends Q with extra Dolev-Yao strands on abstract keys such that if the intruder was able to generate or learn some QKey k from protocol P, then Q^α can generate the abstract version $\alpha(k)$, e.g., a Dolev-Yao strand of the form $:: r :: [nil \mid k_1(i, A, r), \; nil]$ or $[nil \mid + (c), \; nil]$.

The key abstraction α is homomorphically extended to terms. We denote by $t\alpha$ the term $t[\alpha(t_1), \ldots, \alpha(t_n)]_{Pos_1, \ldots, Pos_n}$ where $\{t_1, \ldots, t_n\}$ is the set of top QKey subterms, and $Pos_i = \{p_{ij} \in Pos(t) \mid t|_{p_{ij}} =_{E_P \cup B_P} t_i\}$. Note that it is possible that a QKey term can contain other QKey terms as subterms, but we do not need to consider those subterms that are not at the top QKey position, since Q is parameterized by sort QKey.

Example 9. Consider the key abstraction map α of Example 8 and the following strand Str in a state of protocol $BAC;_\rho PA$:

$$[-(\mathcal{E}(read, f_1(key(reader, r_1), key(passport, r_2)), f_2(key(reader, r_1), key(passport, r_2))))]$$

The result of applying α to Str is:

$$[-(\mathcal{E}(read, k_1(reader, passport, r_1), k_2(reader, passport, r_2)))]$$

Note that for the sake of brevity, encapsulation operator $\mathcal{E}$ has not been expanded into its definition in this example.

We now define the simulation relation $\mathcal{H}_Q$ between $P;_\rho Q$ and Q^α and our main result of this section.

Definition 4 (Relation $\mathcal{H}_Q$). *Let $S_i = SS_i \& IK_i$ denote a state that is reachable from the initial state in protocol $P;_\rho Q$, $S_{Q^\alpha} = SS_{Q^\alpha} \& IK_{Q^\alpha}$ denote a state that is reachable from the initial state in protocol Q^α with α being an admissible* QKey *abstraction, $S_i|_Q$ denote $SS_i|_Q \& IK_i|_{\Sigma_{Q^\rho}}$, and $SS|_Q \& IK|_Q = (S_i|_Q)\alpha$. Let $B_{Q^\alpha} = B_Q \cup B_\alpha$. The relation $\mathcal{H}_Q$ between states in $P;_\rho Q$ and in Q^α is defined by the following equivalence: $(S_i, S_{Q^\alpha}) \in \mathcal{H}_Q$ iff: (i) $SS|_Q \subseteq_{E_Q \cup B_{Q^\alpha}} SS_{Q^\alpha}$, $SS|_{Q,HS} =_{E_Q \cup B_{Q^\alpha}} SS_{Q^\alpha}|_{HS}$, and (ii) $IK|_Q =_{E_Q \cup B_{Q^\alpha}} IK_{Q^\alpha}$.*

The main intuition of the simulation is that since the key abstraction α preserves the equality and deducibility of keys of sort QKey, the protocol Q^α can simulate Q^ρ by taking the same transitions, except that the keys of sort QKey are abstracted according to α.

Theorem 3. *Given a secrecy enforcing key establishment protocol P, a key application protocol Q, the composed protocol $P;_\rho Q$, and an admissible* QKey *abstraction α, if a state S_i is reachable from the initial state of protocol $P;_\rho Q$, then there exists a state S_{Q^α} such that S_{Q^α} is reachable from the initial state in protocol Q^α, and $(S_i, S_{Q^\alpha}) \in \mathcal{H}_Q$.*

From Theorem 3 we can conclude that, if the intruder cannot learn the secret payload message between two honest principals in protocol Q^α, then the composed protocol $P;_\rho Q$ also satisfies this property.

5   Modular Verification of $P;_\rho Q$ in Maude-NPA

In this section we show how the simulation results in Sect. 4 can be used in Maude-NPA's protocol analysis. Given an attack state pattern Att_i of protocol $P;_\rho Q$, we must obtain an attack state pattern Att_P for protocol P (according to Theorem 2) and an attack state pattern Att_Q for protocol Q^α (according to Theorem 3). However, an attack state pattern Att_i may not include any strands of P and we need a completion mechanism, which expands a given attack state pattern so that each child strand in the attack state pattern has a parent strand that is explicitly listed in the state. Following the semantics of sequential protocol composition in Maude-NPA [15], the composition completion of an attack pattern does not change the reachability of the attack pattern.

Definition 5 (Composition Completion). *Given an attack state pattern Att_i of protocol $P;_\rho Q$, w.l.o.g assume that the strands which are instances of strands in protocol Q in Att_i have the form:*

$$Att_i|_Q = (b_1)\ [\{a_1 \rightarrow b_1 ;;\ Mode_1 ;; M_{b_1}\}, L_{b_1} \mid nil]\ \&\ldots\&$$
$$(b_n)\ [\{a_n \rightarrow b_n ;;\ Mode_n ;; M_{b_n}\}, L_{b_n} \mid nil]$$

where $\forall i \in [1, n]$, (b_i) $[\{a_i \to b_i \;;\; Mode_i \;;\; M_{b_i}\}, L_{b_i}]$ *is an instance of a (possibly partial) honest protocol strand of protocol* Q^ρ, *and all the QKeys in* L_{b_i} *show up in* M_{b_i}. *The composition completion of* $Att_;$ *is* $\widehat{Att}_; = \{\widehat{Att}_{;1}, \ldots \widehat{Att}_{;m}\}$ *with* $\widehat{Att}_{;j\in[1,m]} = (Att_;\&Att_P)\theta_j$, *where* Att_P *is defined as follows:*

$$Att_P = (a_1)\; [L_{a_1}, \{a_1 \to b_1 \;;\; Mode_1 \;;\; M_{a_1}\} \mid nil]\; \&\ldots\; \&$$
$$(a_m)\; [L_{a_n}, \{a_n \to b_n \;;\; Mode_n \;;\; M_{a_n}\} \mid nil]$$

where $\forall i \in [1, n]$, (a_i) $[nil | L_{a_i}, \{a_i \to b_i \;;\; Mode_i \;;\; M_{a_i}\}, nil] \in \mathcal{P}_{P;_\rho Q} \cup Att_; |_P$, $\theta_j \in Unif_{E_P \cup B_P}(M_{a_1} = M_{b_1} \land \ldots \land M_{a_n} = M_{b_n})$. *We require that all the QKeys in* $\widehat{Att}_;$ *are instances of the key patterns.*

Example 10. Consider the following attack pattern in the protocol $BAC;_\rho PA$ querying whether the intruder can learn $data(passport, r')$ generated by the passport in the PA protocol:

$$Att_; = [nil, \{BAC.P \to PA.P \;;\; 1{-}1 \;;\; passport; reader; K_1; K_2\}, -(\mathcal{E}(read, K_1, K_2)),$$
$$+ (\mathcal{E}(data(passport, r'); sign(h(data(passport, r')), sk(passport)), K_1, K_2)) \mid nil]$$
$$\&\; data(passport, r') \in \mathcal{I}$$

where K_1 and K_2 denote the key terms $f_1(key(reader, r_1), key(passport, r_2))$ and $f_2(key(reader, r_1), key(passport, r_2))$ respectively. The composition completion is $\widehat{Att}_; = Str_P \& Att_;[P \mapsto passport, R \mapsto reader, K_R \mapsto key(reader, r_1)]$ where Str_P denotes the passport strand in Example 4. Note that the unification call between the input and output synchronization messages gave also some instantiation for P and, thus, we use L_P to denote $Str_P[P \mapsto passport, R \mapsto reader, K_R \mapsto key(reader, r_1)]$. Note that in the case where two participants of a protocol P can swap roles in protocol Q, the unification of the input and output synchronization messages will produce all different combinations.

Given an attack state pattern $Att_;$ in the protocol $P;_\rho Q$, we follow the following steps to check whether the attack state pattern $Att_;$ can backwards reach an initial state in protocol $P;_\rho Q$:

1. *Composition Completion*: we first generate the composition completion $\widehat{Att}_; = \{\widehat{Att}_{;1}, \ldots \widehat{Att}_{;m}\}$ of $Att_;$.
2. For each composition completed state $\widehat{Att}_{;j} = SS_; \& IK_;$ in $\widehat{Att}_;$, we analyze the reachability of $\widehat{Att}_{;j}$ as follows:
   (a) *Reachability in P*: check the attack pattern $S_P = SS_;|_P \& IK_;|_{\Sigma_P(X)}$ in protocol P. If S_P cannot backwards reach an initial state, skip the step (b), and mark the reachability of the state $\widehat{Att}_{;j}$ as false.
   (b) *Reachability in Q^α*: check the attack pattern $S_Q = (SS_;|_Q \& IK_;|_{\Sigma_{Q^\rho}(X)})\alpha$ in protocol Q^α. If S_Q cannot backwards reach an initial state, mark the reachability of the state $\widehat{Att}_{;j}$ as false.

If the reachability of all the states in $\widehat{Att}_i$ are marked as false, then the attack state Att_i cannot reach an initial state, i.e., the protocol $P;_\rho Q$ is secure with respect to the attack state Att_i. Note that extra analysis may be executed in P in order to generate some specific key abstraction mappings.

This approach is indicated in the following theorem. The proof is based on lifting Theorems 1 and 3 to symbolic backwards semantics according to [9].

Theorem 4 (Symbolic Modular Verification Theorem). *Given a key establishment protocol P, a key application protocol Q with key abstraction α, the composed protocol $P;_\rho Q$, and a symbolic attack state Att_i of protocol $P;_\rho Q$, if Att_i can backwards reach an initial state in protocol $P;_\rho Q$, then there exists a state $\widehat{Att}_{i \cdot j} = SS_i \& IK_i$ in the composition completion of Att_i, such that the state $S_P = SS_i|_P \& IK_i|_{\Sigma_P(X)}$ can backwards reach an initial state in P, and the state $S_{Q^\alpha} = (SS_i|_Q \& IK_i|_{\Sigma_{Q^P}(X)})\alpha$ can backwards reach an initial state in Q^α.*

Example 11. As an example of modular protocol analysis, we continue with the protocol $BAC;_\rho PA$ and Example 10.

We first check that the protocol BAC is secrecy enforcing, therefore the intruder cannot learn K_1 or K_2. We then check that in protocol BAC the attack state pattern in which the strand L_P finished execution. Maude-NPA found an initial state, we therefore need to check the reachability in PA^α.

To generate the key abstraction α, we also check in protocol BAC the attack pattern in which the passport's (resp. reader's) strand finished execution without the corresponding reader's (resp. passport's) strand (an authentication attack). Maude-NPA terminated without reaching any initial states. We therefore obtain protocol PA^α from PA by removing the input synchronization message and replacing the two keys by $k_1(R, P, R_r)$ and $k_2(R, P, R_p)$ respectively with R_r, R_p of sort Fresh?, a super sort of Fresh which has no restrictions on unification. The attack pattern of Example 10 is now written according to the key abstraction α and the specification of protocol PA^α as:

$$[nil, -(\mathcal{E}(read, k_1(reader, passport, r_1), k_2(reader, passport, r_2)),$$
$$+ (\mathcal{E}(data(passport, r'); sign(h(data(passport, r')), sk(passport)),$$
$$k_1(reader, passport, r_1), k_2(reader, passport, r_2))) \mid nil] \& data(passport, r') \in \mathcal{I}$$

Maude-NPA terminated without finding any initial states, i.e., this attack cannot happen. We therefore conclude that the intruder cannot learn the secret payload.

6   Examples

In this section we describe some experiments that we have performed[1] using the Maude-NPA cryptographic protocol analysis tool.

---

[1] Available at http://personales.upv.es/sanesro/Maude-NPA-channel/.

BAC-PA. The basic access control protocol (BAC) and passive authentication protocol (PA) are used in E-passport to protect the content of the RFID chip. The session keys established by the BAC protocol are used for secure further communication. The BAC protocol starts with a challenge which is then followed by a mutually authenticated communication between the passport and the reader. One of the protocols that can use the secure communication established by the BAC protocol is the PA protocol. The PA protocol protects the integrity of the content stored in the chip by first hashing the data and then being signed by the Document Signers.

We used Maude-NPA to search for the attack state in which the intruder can learn the stored data from the communication of an honest passport and an honest reader. We first analyze in the protocol BAC alone whether the intruder can learn the generated session keys from an honest passport and reader. Maude-NPA terminated without any attack being found. We therefore analyze in the protocol PA with an admissible key abstraction whether the intruder can learn the stored data assuming the honest session keys being secure. For this property, Maude-NPA terminated without any attack being found. We then can conclude that the intruder cannot learn the stored data from communications using the composition of the protocols BAC and PA. Note that although the BAC protocol can be cracked by brute-force key search, that is an attack that is out of the scope of this analysis tool.

BAC-AA. The session keys established in the BAC protocol can also be used to secure communications in the Active Authentication (AA) protocol, which prevents passport cloning. The protocol AA starts when the reader sends a challenge through a secure communication to the passport. After receiving the challenge, the passport chip generates its own random string, concatenates it with the received challenge, signs the concatenated message with its signing key and sends it back to the reader.

We used Maude-NPA to search for the attack state in which the intruder can learn the stored data or the signing key of a passport. Since we already verified that the intruder cannot learn the honest session keys generated by the BAC protocol, we therefore analyze in the protocol AA with an admissible key abstraction that the intruder cannot learn the stored data or the signing key assuming the honest session keys being secure. For this property, Maude-NPA terminated without any attack being found.

IKEv1. The Internet Key Exchange (IKE) is a protocol suite in IPSec that establishes session keys for protecting the remainder of the sessions. There are two phases in IKE, where Phase 1 generates a key $SKEYID$ that is used to generate three keys $SKEYID_a$, $SKEYID_e$ and $SKEYID_d$ that are passed to the Phase 2 protocol. Phase 1 is in turn divided into two modes, Main Mode, in which identities are always encrypted, and Aggressive Mode, in which they are not. The Phase 2 mode called Quick Mode is used to generate session keys.

There are many ways to mix and match the protocols, which greatly increases the complexity of formal analysis. So the ability to analyze the Phase 1 and Phase 2 protocols separately would be preferable. As an example, we experimented with the Aggressive Mode with digital signatures (AM) and the Quick mode without perfect forward secrecy (QM) in IKE version 1. To check that the intruder cannot learn the generated session key, we first check in a slightly simplified version of the AM protocol that the key $SKEYID$ exchanged between honest participants cannot be learned by the intruder. For this property, Maude-NPA terminated without any attack being found. We were able to find the authentication attack that is mentioned by Cremers in [8], in which Alice may think that she shared a key with Bob, but Bob actually did not accept that key. Although this authentication property failed, the intruder still cannot learn or forge that key. Thus our composition result can be applied.

We then check in QM with an admissible key abstraction that if the keys $SKEYID_a$, $SKEYID_e$ and $SKEYID_d$ generated by honest principles cannot be learned by the intruder, then the secrets that are used for constructing the final session keys cannot be learned by the intruder. Maude-NPA terminated without any attack being found for this property. Therefore the session keys generated by honest principles using this QM following AM is secure.

7   Related Work

The earliest work on modular verification of composed security protocols concentrated on *parallel* composition of protocols, in which two or more protocols run in parallel but are not (or at least not intentionally) sharing any data. Conditions that make modular parallel composition possible, and that can be verified on the protocols running in isolation, were set forth by Guttman and Thayer in [12]. Later work by Cortier et al. in [7] develops syntactically checkable conditions that guarantee modular parallel composition.

One of the most important applications of modular verification, however, is the case of *sequential composition*, in which one protocol (the parent) provides information such as keys, that are used by another protocol (the child). Generally, results in this area describe a set of (mostly syntactic) conditions on parent and child to ensure that the two protocols do not interfere with each other, and a set of security properties, so that, if the conditions are satisfied, and parent and child each satisfy a security property separately, then so does the sequential composition. Modeling of this type of composition is generally done in one of two ways. One, also referred to as *vertical composition* in [11], is to think of the parent protocol as providing *secure channels* through which the child protocol communicates. The other is to have the parent protocol provide keys and other information directly to the child protocol.

Work on composition via channels includes that of Mödersheim et al. [11,14] and that of Cheval et al. [3]. Mödersheim et al. do not impose explicit syntactic conditions on the composed protocols; instead they require that the protocols be secure under parallel composition, which can be verified either syntactically or non-syntactically. This allows them to reason about such constructs as self-composition. Cheval et al. do put syntactic conditions on the composed protocols, and also make use of a construct called an *encapsulation*, which is a term constructed via cryptographic operations on inherited keys, which is a concrete representation of a secure channel. Encapsulations have multiple uses: they protect keys, guarantee that child and parent cannot be confused with each other, and, by providing authentication and confidentiality functionality, proved concrete representations of secure channels. In our work we show that they can be useful for modular verification for composition via inheritance as well.

Work on modular verification for composition via inheritance, to which our work belongs, includes [1,2,4–6,13]. Like ours, these works concentrate on showing that, assuming certain syntactic conditions are satisfied, then, if the individual protocols satisfy certain security properties, the composed protocol satisfies a certain security property. These properties range from very specific (e.g. the security properties satisfied by a PKI in [4]) to very broad (e.g. the secrecy and authentication properties covered in [13]). However, none of them go as far as our work, in which we use simulation to prove results about reachability properties in general. In addition we note that, although [1] offers tool support via Scyther, and [2,4–6] extend to equational theories, to the best of our knowledge ours is the first work to both support equational theories and offer tool support.

8   Conclusion and Future Work

We have presented a method for modular verification of sequentially composed protocols that enables verification of reachability properties that can be decomposed into reachability properties for the component protocols. In addition, our work both supports equational theories and offers tool support.

The constructs we rely on most in our work are the notion of encapsulation from [3], which enforces conditions we need to prove our modularity result, and the sequential composition mechanism used by Maude-NPA, which gives us a semantics for composition. These constructs suggest two ways in which we can extend our results. The first is to take advantage of the properties of encapsulation exploited in [3] to explicitly define the properties of the channels used by the child protocol. This will simplify the analysis of the child protocol even further. The second is to extend our work to support arbitrary composition via global mutable state as in [13]. This would require an extension of the Maude-NPA sequential composition semantics, but not an extension of the tool itself, since automated analysis would be done on the component protocols separately.

References

1. Andova, S., Cremers, C.J.F., Gjøsteen, K., Mauw, S., Mjølsnes, S.F., Radomirovic, S.: A framework for compositional verification of security protocols. Inf. Comput. **206**(2–4), 425–459 (2008)
2. Arapinis, M., Cheval, V., Delaune, S.: Composing security protocols: from confidentiality to privacy. In: Focardi, R., Myers, A. (eds.) POST 2015. LNCS, vol. 9036, pp. 324–343. Springer, Heidelberg (2015). https://doi.org/10.1007/978-3-662-46666-7_17
3. Cheval, V., Cortier, V., le Morvan, E.: Secure refinements of communication channels. In: 35th IARCS Annual Conference on Foundation of Software Technology and Theoretical Computer Science, FSTTCS 2015, India (2015)
4. Cheval, V., Cortier, V., Warinschi, B.: Secure composition of PKIs with public key protocols. In: CSF 2017. Santa Barbara, USA, pp. 144–158 (2017)
5. Chevalier, C., Delaune, S., Kremer, S., Ryan, M.D.: Composition of password-based protocols. Form. Methods Syst. Des. **43**(3), 369–413 (2013)
6. Ciobâcă, Ş., Cortier, V.: Protocol composition for arbitrary primitives. In: CSF 2010, Edinburgh, United Kingdom, pp. 322–336 (2010)
7. Cortier, V., Delaune, S.: Safely composing security protocols. Form. Methods Syst. Des. **34**(1), 1–36 (2009)
8. Cremers, C.: Key exchange in IPsec revisited: formal analysis of IKEv1 and IKEv2. In: Atluri, V., Diaz, C. (eds.) ESORICS 2011. LNCS, vol. 6879, pp. 315–334. Springer, Heidelberg (2011). https://doi.org/10.1007/978-3-642-23822-2_18
9. Escobar, S., Meadows, C., Meseguer, J., Santiago, S.: A rewriting-based forwards semantics for Maude-NPA. In: Proceedings of the 2014 Symposium and Bootcamp on the Science of Security, HotSoS 2014. ACM (2014)
10. Fabrega, F.J.T., Herzog, J., Guttman, J.: Strand spaces: what makes a security protocol correct? J. Comput. Secur. **7**, 191–230 (1999)
11. Groß, T., Mödersheim, S.: Vertical protocol composition. In: CSF 2011. Cernay-la-Ville, France, pp. 235–250 (2011)
12. Guttman, J.D., Thayer, F.J.: Protocol independence through disjoint encryption. In: CSFW, pp. 24–34 (2000)
13. Hess, A.V., Mödersheim, S.A., Brucker, A.D.: Stateful protocol composition. In: Lopez, J., Zhou, J., Soriano, M. (eds.) ESORICS 2018. LNCS, vol. 11098, pp. 427–446. Springer, Cham (2018). https://doi.org/10.1007/978-3-319-99073-6_21
14. Mödersheim, S., Viganò, L.: Sufficient conditions for vertical composition of security protocols. In: Proceedings of the 9th ACM Symposium on Information, Computer and Communications Security, ASIA CCS 2014, pp. 435–446. ACM (2014)
15. Santiago, S., Escobar, S., Meadows, C.A., Meseguer, J.: Effective sequential protocol composition in Maude-NPA. CoRR abs/1603.00087 (2016)

A Spark Is Enough in a Straw World: A Study of Websites Password Management in the Wild

Simone Raponi(✉) and Roberto Di Pietro

College of Science and Engineering, Hamad Bin Khalifa University, Doha, Qatar
{sraponi,rdipietro}@hbku.edu.qa

Abstract. The widespread usage of password authentication in online websites leads to an ever-increasing concern, especially when considering the possibility for an attacker to recover the user password by leveraging the loopholes in the password recovery mechanisms. Indeed, the adoption of a poor password management system by a website makes useless even the most robust password chosen by its users.

In this paper, we first provide an analysis of currently adopted password recovery mechanisms. Later, we model an attacker with a set of different capabilities, and we show how current password recovery mechanisms can be exploited in our attacker model. Then, we provide a thorough analysis of the password management of some of the Alexa's top 200 websites in different countries, including England, France, Germany, Spain and Italy. Of these 1,000 websites, 722 do not require authentication—and hence are excluded from our study—, while out of the remaining 278 we focused on 174—since 104 demanded information we could not produce. Of these 174, almost 25% have critical vulnerabilities, while 44% have some form of vulnerability. Finally, we point out that, by considering the entry into force of the General Data Protection Regulation (GDPR) in May, 2018, most of websites are not compliant with the legislation and may incur in heavy fines. This study, other than being important on its own since it highlights some severe current vulnerabilities and proposes corresponding remedies, has the potential to have a relevant impact on the EU industrial ecosystem.

Keywords: Authentication mechanism · Password recovery · Security

1 Introduction

The countless attacks on websites in recent years have underlined once again that security is often considered a feature, rather than a necessity [15]. The victims of such attacks are the users that, unaware of the management of the provided confidential information, will find their identity and data compromised on the web. In fact, even if a user would adopt all known good practices to choose a really strong password to enforce access control, a single website that

© Springer Nature Switzerland AG 2018
S. K. Katsikas and C. Alcaraz (Eds.): STM 2018, LNCS 11091, pp. 37–53, 2018.
https://doi.org/10.1007/978-3-030-01141-3_3

stores information in an insecure way would be enough to compromise (at least) confidentiality of the provided data. Examples are the data breaches suffered by both the professional networking site LinkedIn [2] and the Internet service company Yahoo [5]. LinkedIn suffered a major breach in June 2012, when 6.5 million encrypted passwords were posted on a Russian website. Things got much worse in May 2016, when 117 million LinkedIn credentials (i.e., combination of e-mails and passwords) were posted for sale on the Dark Web [1]. Although LinkedIn was a well-known and well-established website, poor cryptography techniques were implemented [23], by making easier for hackers to decrypt users' passwords. The attack targeting Yahoo was the biggest one in history, which led to the breach of 3 billion passwords. The hack began with a spear-phishing e-mail sent to a Yahoo employee, that eventually led to the acquisition of the entire users database by the attacker (containing names, phone numbers, password challenge questions and answers, password recovery e-mails and a cryptographic value unique to each account) [8]. If it were true that history taught, we should have solved (or at least mitigated) problems of this kind, but reality is different. In fact, in this work we point out that almost 44% of the top Alexa's websites we considered (out of the top 200 of respectively England, France, Germany, Italy, and Spain, shown in Table 3) do store users password in a form that can be easily exploited. While the impact of these findings are relevant on their own, their consequences for companies are magnified when taking into account the GDPR—the poor security measures adopted by the web sites are a clear violation of.

The General Data Protection Regulation (GDPR) [6] leads to an important change in the vision of both data privacy and data security. Born as an evolution of the previous Data Protection Directive, adopted in 1995, it became enforceable since May 25th, 2018. With its entry into force, all the websites, agencies, enterprises, organizations, that make use of the personal data of the users have to guarantee their protection both by design and default in any operation. In case of non-compliance, these entities are subject to very heavy penalties ranging from 10–20 million euros to 2–4% of the annual worldwide turnover of the previous financial year, unsustainable by most organizations.

Contributions. In this paper we first provide an analysis of both users authentication mechanisms implemented by websites and related password recovery mechanisms. Then we model a realistic attacker with different capabilities, respectively Mail Service Provider attacker, Web Server Intruder attacker, Client Intruder attacker, and Sniffing attacker. Later we provide a thorough analysis for users password management Alexa's top 200 websites of the five aforementioned European countries. Then, we study in detail which information could be obtained by our modeled attacker and we show how she can break the access control mechanisms.

Results are striking; of the 174 analyzed websites (see Table 3) almost 25% of the websites do have from poor to very poor password management, and an overall of 43.68% are vulnerable to at least one of the presented attacks—note that all the attacks happen because of the non-compliance of the websites to the GDPR prescriptions, hence having the corresponding organizations being subject to the cited fines.

Road-Map: In Sect. 2, we report on the related work in the literature. In Sect. 3, we provide a technical background of both user authentication on websites and the password recovery mechanisms. In Sect. 4, we define our attacker model. In Sect. 5, we describe the methodology we adopted and we present the results of the analysis, while in Sect. 6 we report some concluding remarks.

2   Related Work

LinkedIn data breaches in June 2012 [2] and Yahoo data breaches in August 2013 [5], made respectively 6.5 million and 3 billion users accounts compromised, but these compromises are only the tip of the iceberg. However, these attacks have not affected the popularity of passwords. In fact, passwords remain the most widespread authentication mechanism on the web. The use of a password introduces a secret that is shared by only the authenticator (the website), and the user wishing to be authenticated.

From the moment they were adopted, a number of scientific articles were published with the aim of highlighting their weaknesses and vulnerabilities. In [18] the authors analyzed half a million Windows Live users' passwords, pointing out that a user has 6.5 passwords shared across 3.9 different sites on average. Furthermore, each user is the owner of about 25 accounts and types an average of 8 passwords per day. Most of the picked passwords are extremely weak, in fact, if not forced, users choose passwords composed by solely lowercase letters. Dell'Amico et al., in [17] focused on the empirical study of real-world passwords. They implemented and used several state-of-the-art techniques for password guessing to analyze the password strength of Internet application. They found that users put relatively little effort in choosing their password when compared to the choice of their usernames. The human component plays a fundamental role in both the security and the robustness of the authentication mechanisms. Indeed, even the most advanced system would be compromised if users pay little attention to their password choice.

Passwords authentication mechanisms will still be used for years, as "something you know" mechanisms are extremely less expensive (but also less secure) than both "something you have" and "something you are"—these latter ones being prone also to false positive and false negative. By considering this, it is of fundamental importance to guarantee both secure access and secure storage, as well as secure mechanism to retrieve the password in case of forgetfulness or theft. In [19], the authors presented an assessment of password practices on 10 popular websites, including Facebook, Amazon, Yahoo, Google, and YouTube. They examined password selection, the restrictions enforced on password choice, and the recovery/reset of the password if forgotten. They pointed out that no website provides adequate coverage of all the criteria taken into account. The result is worrying, as the websites analyzed are among the most visited on the web and therefore (should be) the safest.

When we lose or forget our passwords we generally use our e-mail address to retrieve them, assuming that we are the only ones who have the access. Garfinkel, in [21], wondered if an e-mail-based Identification and Authentication (EBIA) method could substitute the Public Key Infrastructure (PKI). The EBIA technique considers an e-mail address as a universal identifier and the ability to receive an e-mail at that address as a kind of authenticator. Among the many limitations, the author pointed out two many vulnerabilities: EBIA security strongly depends on the security of e-mail servers and password; e-mail content is accessible to server operators (without encryption, system managers can intercept, read, and make copies of e-mail messages intended for end users). Although the paper is dated back 2003, EBIA is the main used secondary (also known as emergency) authentication method nowadays, with the same vulnerabilities (and a few additional ones) left unresolved. One possible countermeasure would be to use secure e-mail services, such as ProtonMail [10]. ProtonMail is an open-source end-to-end encrypted e-mail service founded in 2014 at the CERN. This service allows to protect the user's privacy and anonymity by not logging IP addresses which can be linked to the account, furthermore the end-to-end encryption makes unreadable the e-mail content even to the mail provider.

In recent years, various alternatives were proposed to manage the secondary authentication mechanism in a safer way. After "something you have", "something you are", and "something you know", in [16] the authors explored a fourth-factor authentication: "somebody you know". They focused in a process called vouching, a peer-level authentication in which a user (called helper), leverages her primary authenticator to assist a second user (called asker) to perform secondary authentication. They designed a prototype vouching system for SecurID, a hardware authentication token, to allow an helper to grant temporary access privileges to an asker who has lost the ability to use her own. Although interesting, this method requires a primary authentication mechanism based on token, hence "something you have", which is not implemented by most web sites. In [27] Schechter et al. exploited the social-authentication to let users who have forgotten their passwords to regain access to their account. The proposed system employs trustees, users previously appointed by account holders to verify their identity. To get the access into her account, the account holder contacts their trustees in person or by phone, so that their trustees may recognize her by either her appearance or her voice. Once the recognition has occurred, the trustees provide the account holder with an account recovery code, that will be necessary to authenticate her in the system. This mechanism is safer with respect to the ones currently adopted but may have usability problems. Trustees may not be available at the time of request, making it impossible to the requesting user to recover her account.

The secondary authentication mechanisms are discussed and analyzed in [26]. In this work the authors considered four key criteria (i.e., reliability, security, authentication, and setup efficiency) to evaluate several secondary authentication mechanisms, such as security questions, printed shared secrets, previously used passwords, e-mail-based verification, phones or other services, trustees, and in-person proofing. Although they provided a thorough analysis of these mechanisms, no attackers were modeled and no experimental website security analysis was performed.

3   Technical Background

In this section, a technical background of both user authentication mechanisms on websites and password recovery mechanisms adopted by websites are provided.

3.1   User Authentication on Websites

With user authentication on websites we refer to the process by which the credentials provided by the user are compared to those stored either in websites database or in a cloud server. If the credentials match, the authentication process is completed and the requesting user is granted authorization to access. According to the website policy, a few user authentication methods can be implemented [20]. A combination of these methods leads to a more accurate identification of the user:

- **1FA**: the 1-Factor-Authentication (1FA) method requires only one factor to authenticate a user. Usually it takes into account "something the user knows" (e.g., a password or a PIN code). 1FA is the authentication mechanism most commonly adopted by the current websites;
- **2FA**: the 2-Factor-Authentication (2FA) method requires two factors to authenticate a user. It takes into account both "something the user knows" and either "something the user has" (e.g., physical token or a smart card) or "something the user is" (e.g., fingerprints, retinal or iris scans, voice recognition, hand geometry). This mechanism is adopted in most of the sensitive websites (e.g., bank websites) and is optional in others (e.g., Gmail [13], ProtonMail [11]);
- **3FA**: the 3-Factor-Authentication (3FA) method requires a user being authenticated with "something she knows" as well as with both "something she has" and "something she is". This mechanism has not been adopted by the websites, probably due to the infrastructure costs that would derive from it.

3.2   Password Recovery

Password recovery is a mechanism implemented by websites that allows to recover the user's secret password in case the password is lost or forgotten. During the years, numerous mechanisms have been proposed to recover the password, the most frequently adopted are reported below.

Security Questions. When the account holder loses or forgets her password, the password recovery mechanism starts up and provides the user with security questions. This mechanism is based on the assumption that only the account holder is able to answer correctly. Some websites make use of a set of pre-packaged standard questions, while others allow the users to choose their own. In each case, several work demonstrated both limits and vulnerabilities of this mechanism. Using a set of pre-packaged password is quite insecure in the era of the information; answering questions like "what is the name of your primary school?" or "what is your favorite movie?" becomes trivial by having access to all the personal information the user shares on social networks. On the contrary, users could choose their own customized security questions. Even in this case, several work [22,26] demonstrated how weak the mechanism is. As they mention, users should select questions that are memorable, not researchable on-line, reasonably unpopular with other users, and unknown by any untrusted acquaintances.

Previously Used Passwords. Websites, as a password recovery mechanism, could ask the user to enter one (or a set of) previously used password(s). However, users tend to use a limited number of passwords for the web services they access, this phenomenon leading to the unavoidable use of the same password for one or more services. Given that, it should be easy for users to remember one of the password previously used—with high probability it will be a password they are currently using for another web service. Although with both some limitations (e.g., the user may not remember any of the previous passwords) and many security problems (e.g., the attacker may know some of the previous passwords of the victim) the adoption of this method would be less dangerous than the ones currently implemented. It is worth noting that this method cannot be applied if the password has been lost or stolen for the first time.

E-mail-Based Authentication. The most common password recovery mechanism is the e-mail-based authentication, which relies on the assumption that only the account holder will be able to access a secret sent to her e-mail account [21,26]. As we will discuss in Sect. 5, websites can provide the requesting user with her credential information in several ways:

- sending the old password by e-mail;
- sending a new password by e-mail (temporary or not);
- sending an HTTP link by e-mail (to choose a new password); or
- sending an HTTPS link by e-mail (to choose a new password).

The vulnerabilities of this mechanism are detailed in Sect. 5.

Other Password Recovery Mechanisms. Many alternatives have been proposed to manage the password recovery mechanisms in a safer way. Mobiles can be used for user authentication: the website can send users an SMS message or use an automated voice system to call them and provide an account recovery code. As for e-mail-based authentication, this alternative relies on the fact that only the device holder will be able to access a secret that has been sent to the device [26]. Brainard et al., in [16], rely on *trustees*, users previously appointed by the account holder, necessary to verify her identity. These people will be contacted in case of emergency (the password is either lost or compromised) and they will be asked to perform the recognition of the requesting user. If the recognition phase is successful they will provide the requesting user with a recovery code, useful to authenticate her on the website.

4   Adversary Model

Given the websites ecosystem, we consider several categories of adversaries. An adversary may be *undetectable* or *detectable.* An undetectable adversary is able to impersonate the user on websites without the victim being aware of it. Conversely, a detectable adversary impersonating the user has a chance of getting the user being aware, or a least suspicious, of the fact that an impersonation happened (or could have happened). An adversary may also be *active* or *passive.* An active attacker interacts with websites in order to get information about the victim (e.g., she can start the recovery procedure on behalf of the victim), while a passive attacker aims to obtain the target user's sensitive information without any interaction with the website. Eventually, both active and passive attackers can use the obtained information to access websites by pretending to be the victim. Remembering these distinctions (summarized in Table 1), we introduce four different possible attacks against a single target user, taking into account a single target website:

- Mail service provider-level attack;
- Web server intruder attack;
- Client intruder attack;
- Sniffing attack.

Table 1. Attackers types

Type	Detectable	Undetectable
Active	Can interact with the website on behalf of the victim by revealing her existence	Can interact with the website on behalf of the victim by remaining transparent
Passive	Cannot interact with the website, but her actions will eventually make the victim aware of her existence	Cannot interact with the website and will remain transparent

Table 2. Attackers capabilities

Attackers/access	User e-mails	Website password DB	Website password recovery method
Mail service provider attacker	✓	✗	✓
Web server intruder attacker	✗	✓	✓
Client intruder attacker	✓	✗	✓
Sniffing attacker	✗	✗	✓

A *mail service provider-level attack* can be undertaken by both a malicious service provider, or a malicious user that has compromised the mail service provider. This is the most dangerous attack, as the attacker has access to all the user's e-mails and can obtain a lot of sensitive information. In the *web server intruder attack*, we suppose the attacker was able to violate a website where the user has registered an account. So, the adversary can interact with the database that stores all the passwords of the users. A *client intruder attack* can be undertaken by an adversary that either has violated a user's device by obtaining a remote access, or has stolen it. In the *sniffing attack* we suppose that the attacker has no knowledge about the user, she has neither access to the website's password database nor to the user's devices. The only information she has, is about the password recovery methods of the website (to obtain this information she could register an account and start the recovery procedure). The sniffing adversary can sniff the packets transmitted during the communication between the client and the website. We assume without loss of generality that the sniffing attacker is not able to read the content of the exchanged e-mails (for instance, because the HTTPS protocol is used). The capabilities of attackers are summarized in Table 2.

5   Methodology and Results

In this section we provide the methodology employed to analyze the websites' password management security. The methodology involves two independent choices:

1. which website to take into account for the analysis; and,
2. how to analyze the websites.

As for the first choice, we decided to make use of the Amazon Alexa Top Sites web service [3]. Amazon Alexa Top Sites is a web service that provides a list of websites, ordered by Alexa Traffic Rank. This ranking is determined by a combined measure of both websites' unique visitors and websites' page views, and is updated daily [7]. So, we selected a subset of countries, respectively England, France, Germany, Italy, and Spain according to their subjectiveness to the GDPR regulation—till Brexit happens, UK is subject to GDPR as well. For each of these countries, we considered the first top 200 websites according to Alexa's ranking. The choice of this parameter is due to the fact that as the ranking goes down, the websites become less and less used–hence, with a reduced impact. We have therefore created an account and started obtaining the websites' URLs we needed. Amazon Alexa provides several ways for obtaining websites information; in particular, the top websites can be selected according to three major divisions: global; by country; and by category. The global division, as the name suggests, shows the most visited websites globally. The division by country, instead, allows to view the most visited websites from specific countries, not necessarily with the domain registered in the country taken into account (e.g., the website *youtube.com* is in the top five of all the countries considered in this analysis, but its domain is registered in the US). The third division is the more generic and allows to select the top 200 websites according to different sub-categories (e.g., adult, arts, computers, recreation, regional, sports, and so on). By selecting the regional category, we were able to choose the continent first and then the specific nations we would like to consider. In this case, Alexa shows the top 200 websites for the countries selected, that represents the top 200 websites with the domains registered in those countries. Once obtained the websites URLs, our goal was to analyze them in order to get information about the password storage management. In the second phase we started by selecting, among the top 200 websites for each nation, the ones that required a user registration.

A further filtering step was to remove those websites that, in the user registration phase, required privileged information (e.g., id number for universities, account number for banks, customer code for wholesalers). In detail, of these 1,000 websites, 722 did not require authentication—and hence were excluded by our study—, while out of the remaining 278, we focused on 174—since 104 demanded information we could not produce. The results of this filtering are shown in Table 3.

Table 3. Number of analyzed websites (among the top 200 per country)

Country	Websites (#)
England	71
France	31
Germany	19
Italy	36
Spain	17
Total	**174**

By considering the number of websites, we decided to manually perform the analysis of each one, in order to obtain more accurate and detailed information—while this activity took quite some amount of time (around three months), the quality of results is unpaired. In particular, for each website:

- we registered an user account;
- we pretended to have lost the password and we started the recovery procedure; and,
- we collected password recovery information.

Table 4. Password recovery mechanisms adopted by the analyzed websites

Country	Websites (#)	Old Pw	New Pw	Temp Pw	HTTP link	% of vulnerable websites
England	71	1	5	2	16	33.8
France	31	0	10	0	7	54.84
Germany	19	1	1	0	5	36.84
Italy	36	4	11	1	4	55.55
Spain	17	2	5	0	1	47.06
Total	**174**	**8**	**32**	**3**	**33**	**43.68**

We registered on the websites by using a Gmail account created for the experiment, i.e., *gdpr.experiment@gmail.com*. The results of the analysis are shown in Table 4. Each column of the table represents a different method of password recovery adopted by the analyzed websites—these password recovery methods can be observed from left to right in decreasing order of vulnerability.

5.1 Password Recovery Methods

In the following, we describe each password recovery method adopted by the analyzed websites.

Old Password. The most vulnerable websites are the ones that use the *Old Pw* method for the password recovery phase. In detail, after having completed the "forgotten password" procedure, the website sends the original password of the user in her registration e-mail address. Hence, it appears that websites do not make use of hash functions or other mechanisms in order to avoid to store the passwords in cleartext. Considering that most of the users make use of the same password to access many different services [12], obtaining access to the database of password stored by the website (by an hacker attack or an internal website error) would seriously jeopardize both the security and the privacy of all the registered users. This method of storing password is deprecated since at least 30 years [25].

New Password. In this recovery method, after the "forgotten password" procedure, the website sends a new password to the registration e-mail address of the user, without obliging her to change the password after the first access. The security of passwords sent by using this method is summarized in Table 5. In this analysis we take a lenient stance and consider respectively: *strong* the passwords with at least 2^{70} possible combinations; *medium* the passwords with at least 2^{50} possible combinations; and *weak* all the others. We have obtained this data by requesting a new password 125 times, and by analyzing the type of provided password. For instance, *VUZUK8G3*, *484ad5b5*, *ugrxpn* are three of the passwords provided by a given website following the recovery procedure. It is possible to see that all the passwords use only uppercase or lowercase letters, sometimes numbers, never special characters, with an overall length of 8. In this case, the strength has been computed as $62^8 \approx 2^{48}$.

Table 5. Password robustness analysis

	$>2^{10}$	$>2^{20}$	$>2^{30}$	$>2^{40}$	$>2^{50}$	$>2^{60}$	$>2^{70}$
New	100%	93.75%	75%	62.5%	3.125%	3.125%	3.125%
Temporary	100%	100%	100%	100%	33.33%	0	0

Note that only 3.125% of the new passwords provided to the users by the website have what could be considered a decent level of security, while more than 90% are considered weak. This password choice makes the websites vulnerable to brute-force attacks, where malicious users can try to guess the users' password after requesting the re-sending on behalf of the victims.

Temporary Password. The *Temp Pw* method consists in sending a temporary password to the requesting user, where this password must be changed on her next access. Only few websites make use of this recovery method, and those who do, they send either weak or medium security password to the requester e-mail account (see Table 5).

HTTP Link. Almost 19% of the websites use the *HTTP link* as recovery method. In this case, once the user has requested for the password recovery, the web service sends an HTTP link to her registration e-mail address. By clicking on the link, the requester is redirected to the website on which she can enter a new password that will be associated with her account. We consider vulnerable the websites that make use of this recovery method. Indeed it is well-known that the HTTP protocol does not provide insurance with respect to attacks such as man in the middle [9], or even simple snooping. Considering that all communications between user browser and websites are not encrypted, a malicious user can intercept the message exchange, eavesdrop and modify the communication, compromising both its confidentiality and integrity.

HTTPS Link. The last analyzed recovery method of the websites is the *HTTPS link* one, in which the link sent to the user to let her choose a new password is based on HTTPS protocol. This method is safer with respect to the others but it is subject to being exploited as well, as we will detail in the following.

5.2   Attackers Capabilities

In this section we describe the capabilities of attackers as well as their characteristics. Results of this study are summarized in Table 6 for passive attackers, and in Table 7 for active attackers.

Mail Service Provider-Level Attacker. A *passive mail service provider-level attacker* may obtain the user's log-in information in any case, regardless of the password recovery methods adopted by the website. In fact, this kind of attacker has access to the e-mails of the victim, the emergency authentication mechanisms currently adopted by websites. In case of *Old Pw* or *New Pw* recovery methods, the attacker can even remain undetectable. In fact, by easily reading the password inside the e-mail, the attacker and the victim would share the same account unbeknownst to the latter. The attacker is forced to adopt a detectable method in the other cases (i.e., the adversary can use either the temporary password or both the HTTP and HTTPS link to log-in with the credentials of the victim, but once logged in she is forced to change the password, by no longer granting access to the victim). In this situation, the provider could obtain the credentials (by reading either the new or the temporary password) as well as the links (either HTTP or HTTPS) and destroy the received e-mail. The user would not receive the e-mail but could attribute the fact to a website malfunction. In the meantime, the adversary may have entered, obtained the information she needed, and logged out. There is a good chance of not being suspected at all.

An *active mail service provider-level attacker* could remain undetectable if the target website stores the passwords of registered users in clear. In fact, by starting the recovery procedure, she can obtain the original password of the user by e-mail. This e-mail will be deleted from the system as soon as possible. In all other cases, the password would change and the mail service provider-level attacker will delete the compromising e-mail. The victim would have no longer access to the website but could attribute the fact to either a website malfunction or to having forgotten the password.

Web Server Intruder Attacker. The information that a *passive web server intruder attacker* can gain is strongly dependent on the password storage management of the website she has violated. Indeed, if the passwords of the registered users are stored in clear text (i.e., without the support provided by hash functions), the attacker could transparently make use of the credentials of the victim to access the target website.

The capability does not change from the perspective of an *active web server intruder attacker*, because they would still depend to the storage methods. In addition, note that the victim would be aware of an attack as it would receive e-mails with instructions for recovering the password.

Client Intruder Attacker. A *passive client intruder attacker*, with remote or physical access to the device of the victim, would have most of the time exactly the same capabilities of an mail service provider-level attacker (i.e., there is often no need to insert a password to access services, most of users allow the browser to remember it [28]). Furthermore, either remote or physical access to the device would allow the attacker to find any password file written by the victim [29], so the attacker capabilities depend on the victim's behavior. If the victim does not allow the browser to remember the information about her credentials, an attacker with remote or temporarily physical access to the device could install a key-logger software [24], that would capture user input and provides the attacker the information about the keys typed (including the passwords of the websites that the victim will visit in that session).

An *active client intruder attacker* would have the same capabilities of the active mail service provider-level attacker, because of the same access to the e-mail account of the victim.

Sniffing Attacker. A *passive sniffing attacker* can obtain the access information of a target user mainly in two ways: she can intercept the HTTP communications, as well as undertake a man-in-the-middle attack [9] during an HTTPS communication, or she can try to brute-force a target website until the victim's credentials are guessed [14]. In this case, unless the website implements some type of protection (e.g., CAPTCHA, blocking of the account log-in for a few seconds after n attempts) or warning system (e.g., sending an e-mail to the account owner after a number of failed log-in attempts), the attacker would be undetectable due to her knowledge of the password of the victim.

The capabilities of an *active sniffing attacker*, instead, would be subject to various changes. If the server adopts the old Pw recovery method (e.g., it stores the registered users passwords in clear text and, when requested, it sends back the original user's password), the sniffing attacker can ask for the password recovery on behalf of the user but it would be both detectable (given that the user will receive the e-mail with the old password) and useless (she should brute-force the same password as before). In case the web server adopted either New or Temp Pw password recovery method, instead, the active sniffing attacker would have useful information about the password she has to brute-force. In fact, even if the user has a very strong password, the attacker could apply for a new (or a temp) one on her behalf. In this way, the attacker would know exactly the structure and the level of security of the new website-generated password and could brute-force it accordingly. For example, the target user has a very hard-to-guess password, and the attacker starts the password recovery methods on a target website in her behalf. The attacker, by registering a personal account on that website, knows how temp and new passwords are chosen (e.g., only numbers, both capital letter and numbers, etc.), so she would have useful information about the password structure as well as its length. In case of HTTP or HTTPS links used for password recovery, the attack will become detectable and the attacker would not gain any additional information about the password with respect to the passive attacker ones.

Table 6. Synoptic table related to passive attackers

Attacks/ Recovery methods	Old Pw	New Pw	Temp Pw	HTTP link	HTTPS link
Mail service provider-level	*undetectable*	*undetectable*	*detectable*	*detectable*	*detectable*
Web server intruder	*undetectable*	Depends on the storage method	Depends on the storage method	Depends on the storage method	Depends on the storage method
Client intruder	*undetectable*	*undetectable*	*detectable*/ Depends on the user's behavior	*detectable*/ Depends on the user's behavior	*detectable*/ Depends on the user's behavior
Sniffing	*undetectable*	*undetectable*	*undetectable*	*undetectable*	*undetectable*

Note that two of the main differences between passive and active attackers involve attack timing and attack extension. On the one hand, active attackers may get information about the victim's credentials at any time, while passive ones must wait for a move from the user. On the other hand, an active attacker must take immediate actions while a passive attacker can be implemented as a fragment of autonomous software that will be triggered by certain events (e.g., starting of a recovery password procedure by the user, receiving a mail with credentials/links). This means that passive attacker softwares could be easily and quickly propagated.

Best Practices. The provided analysis has highlighted serious security deficiencies related to the storage and management of websites passwords. This paragraph contains a list of best practices to be used for a first mitigation phase.

Basic security guidelines dictate, for at least 40 years, that passwords should never be stored in clear text. For instance, passwords could be hashed by using a dash of salt, different for each one, making any salted rainbow table useless or extremely slow (because of the prohibitively size) Another solution can be the implementation of slow hashes by websites. The website would suffer negligible delay every time a user registers an account or logs in, but the password table attack by the attacker would be infeasible due to the time required. Moreover, the password length plays a fundamental role. Computers, Field-programmable

Table 7. Synoptic table related to active attackers

Attacks/ Recovery methods	Old Pw	New Pw	Temp Pw	HTTP link	HTTPS link
Mail service provider-level	*undetectable*	*detectable*	*detectable*	*detectable*	*detectable*
Web server intruder	*undetectable*	*detectable*/Depends on the storage method	*detectable*/ Depends on the storage method	*detectable*/ Depends on the storage method	*detectable*/ Depends on the storage method
Client intruder	*undetectable*	*detectable*	*detectable*	*detectable*	*detectable*
Sniffing	*detectable - useless*	*detectable - simpler*	*detectable - simpler*	*detectable*	*detectable*

gate array (FPGA), and Application-specific integrated circuit (ASIC) technologies, are faster, enabling to brute-force both non-salted and salted passwords, if not long enough. 8-character passwords are not enough robust even by using a combination of numbers, lowercase letters, uppercase letters, and special characters. In fact, even by considering a fully random password, the complexity will be equal to 95^8 ($<2^{56}$), a negligible number if we consider that the validation of a block of BitCoin transactions requires, as of writing, 2^{72} hashes [4]. Considering these premises, websites should be able to accept only passwords with an high level of security ($>2^{70}$).

Since currently, for most websites, the ability to access an e-mail address identifies the registered user as the owner of that address, some further good practices could be provided to users:

– do not allow the browsers/websites (especially the mail service providers' ones) to save the password. Better to waste a few seconds to rewrite it than losing control of your identity on the web;
– always log-out from websites and remove open sessions;
– avoid using the same password for more than one website, otherwise check how the passwords are stored (and password recovery are managed) from the website before entering the sensitive password;
– before inserting either passwords or other sensitive information, make sure that there are no key loggers in your system (at least the software ones, more easily detectable);

6   Conclusion

In this paper, we first provided an analysis of both user authentication mechanisms implemented by websites, and password recovery mechanisms currently adopted. Then, we modeled an attacker with a set of capabilities and we showed how simply she is able to get the users' confidential information—e.g. recovering the password, or accessing e-mail. Later, we performed a detailed analysis of users password management for Alexa's top 200 websites (see Sect. 5) of five European countries, respectively England, France, Germany, Italy, and Spain. It is worth noting that analyzed websites are among the top ones according to the Alexa's ranking, so, being the most visited, they are supposed to be way too secure compared to those present in the lower ranking. Our results show that, nowadays, almost 44% of the analyzed websites are vulnerable—simply because lacking adoption of best practices, and hence subject to GDPR's fines. We are currently working on an open-source host-based software that can manage authentication and password recovery from any website in a more secure way, effectively thwarting the discussed attacks.

References

1. 2012 linkedin breach just got a lot worse: 117 million new logins for sale. https://threatpost.com/2012-linkedin-breach-just-got-a-lot-worse-117-million-new-logins-for-sale/118173/. Accessed June 2018
2. 6.5 million linkedin passwords reportedly leaked, linkedin is looking into it. http://goo.gl/dWMvd7. Accessed June 2018
3. Amazon alexa topsites. http://money.cnn.com/2017/10/03/technology/business/yahoo-breach-3-billion-accounts/index.html. Accessed June 2018
4. Blockchain last block. https://blockchain.info/block/0000000000000000001ba3bf33b8c46856dfc05a3b3aebffa245f16269b54dc1. Accessed June 2018
5. Every single yahoo account was hacked - 3 billion in all. https://www.alexa.com/topsites. Accessed June 2018
6. Gdpr portal. https://www.eugdpr.org/. Accessed June 2018
7. How are alexas traffic rankings determined? http://goo.gl/jMjpeS. Accessed June 2018
8. Inside the russian hack of yahoo: How they did it. https://www.csoonline.com/article/3180762/data-breach/inside-the-russian-hack-of-yahoo-how-they-did-it.html. Accessed June 2018
9. Man-in-the-middle attack. https://www.owasp.org/index.php/Man-in-the-middle_attack. Accessed June 2018
10. Protonmail. https://protonmail.com/. Accessed June 2018
11. Protonmail - two factor authentication (2fa). https://protonmail.com/support/knowledge-base/two-factor-authentication/. Accessed June 2018
12. The real life risks of re using the same passwords. https://pixelprivacy.com/resources/reusing-passwords/. Accessed June 2018
13. Stronger security for your google account. https://www.google.com/landing/2step/. Accessed June 2018
14. Using burp to brute force a login page. https://goo.gl/jfwiCJ. Accessed June 2018
15. Website security statistics report. https://info.whitehatsec.com/rs/whitehatsecurity/images/2015-Stats-Report.pdf. Accessed June 2018
16. Brainard, J., Juels, A., Rivest, R.L., Szydlo, M., Yung, M.: Fourth-factor authentication: somebody you know. In: Proceedings of the 13th ACM Conference on Computer and Communications Security, pp. 168–178. ACM (2006)
17. Dell'Amico, M., Michiardi, P., Roudier, Y.: Password strength: an empirical analysis. In: Proceedings of IEEE INFOCOM 2010, pp. 1–9. IEEE (2010)

18. Florencio, D., Herley, C.: A large-scale study of web password habits. In: Proceedings of the 16th International Conference on World Wide Web, pp. 657–666. ACM (2007)
19. Furnell, S.: An assessment of website password practices. Comput. Secur. **26**(7–8), 445–451 (2007)
20. Furnell, S.: A comparison of website user authentication mechanisms. Comput. Fraud Secur. **2007**(9), 5–9 (2007)
21. Garfinkel, S.L.: Email-based identification and authentication: an alternative to PKI? IEEE Secur. Privacy **99**(6), 20–26 (2003)
22. Just, M., Aspinall, D.: Personal choice and challenge questions: a security and usability assessment. In: Proceedings of the 5th Symposium on Usable Privacy and Security, p. 8. ACM (2009)
23. Kamp, P.H., et al.: Linkedin password leak: salt their hide. ACM Queue **10**(6), 20 (2012)
24. Ladakis, E., Koromilas, L., Vasiliadis, G., Polychronakis, M., Ioannidis, S.: You can type, but you can hide: a stealthy GPU-based keylogger. In: Proceedings of the 6th European Workshop on System Security (EuroSec) (2013)
25. Parker, D.B.: Fighting Computer Crime. Scribner, New York (1983)
26. Reeder, R., Schechter, S.: When the password doesn't work: secondary authentication for websites. IEEE Secur. Privacy **9**(2), 43–49 (2011)
27. Schechter, S., Egelman, S., Reeder, R.W.: It's not what you know, but who you know: a social approach to last-resort authentication. In: Proceedings of the SIGCHI Conference on Human Factors in Computing Systems, pp. 1983–1992. ACM (2009)
28. Stobert, E., Biddle, R.: The password life cycle: user behaviour in managing passwords. In: Proceedings of SOUPS (2014)
29. Yan, J., Blackwell, A., Anderson, R., Grant, A.: Password memorability and security: empirical results. IEEE Secur. Privacy **2**(5), 25–31 (2004). https://doi.org/10.1109/MSP.2004.81

A Fast and Scalable Fragmentation Algorithm for Data Protection Using Multi-storage over Independent Locations

Katarzyna Kapusta$^{(\boxtimes)}$ and Gerard Memmi

LTCI, Telecom ParisTech, Paris, France
{katarzyna.kapusta,gerard.memmi}@telecom-paristech.fr

Abstract. Data fragmentation and dispersal over several independent locations enhances protection level of outsourced data. In this paper, we introduce a Fast and Scalable Fragmentation Algorithm (FSFA) that is particularly well adapted to be used in a multi-cloud environment. It transforms data into interdependent fragments that all have to be gathered in order to reconstruct the initial information. A performance comparison with published related works (including data encryption and dispersal) demonstrates it can be more than twice faster than the fastest of the relevant fragmentation techniques, while producing reasonable storage overhead.

Keywords: Data protection · Fragmentation · Information dispersal
Distributed systems · Cloud storage · Multi-cloud · Multi-storage

1 Introduction

Data protection inside cloud-based storage systems remains quite a challenge. Data breaches happen on a daily basis, in extreme cases leading to a massive disclosure of sensitive data[1]. A user uploading their data to the cloud has to trust that the provider will be able to protect the data not only from exterior attackers[2], but also from insider threats such as malicious system administrators or implementation issues. Moreover, the user has to accept the fact that not all Service-Level Agreements (SLAs) reveal in which country data have been stored nor if the data have been reported to a foreign administration or third party.

One way of reinforcing data protection and availability consists in data dispersal over multiple storage locations [3,9,10,15,17] preventing an adversary unable of compromising all the storage domains from acquiring the totality of the data. This concept is getting increasing attention in the context of current developments of the cloud technology enabling data scattering over dozens of

---

[1] https://www.bloomberg.com/news/features/2017-09-29/the-equifax-hack-has-all-the-hallmarks-of-state-sponsored-pros.

[2] https://en.wikipedia.org/wiki/Facebook-Cambridge_Analytica_data_scandal.

© Springer Nature Switzerland AG 2018
S. K. Katsikas and C. Alcaraz (Eds.): STM 2018, LNCS 11091, pp. 54–69, 2018.
https://doi.org/10.1007/978-3-030-01141-3_4

servers situated on independent storage sites [5]. A user not completely trusting their storage providers may want to encrypt the data before dispersal. This
reasonable solution comes with two drawbacks.

First, the user must take care of the key management. A key loss will very
probably make the data unusable (especially in a long-term storage context).
Relying on secure mechanisms may not be sufficient to protect the key from
being acquired as a result, e.g. of using backdoors, coercion, or bribe. An adversary possessing the encryption key and able to compromise some of the storage
sites can decrypt a part of the information. To protect the user against such a
powerful attacker, several solutions based on variations of all-or-nothing transform (AONT) or information dispersal were proposed [13]. They reinforce the
data protection level, but at the cost of performance decrease. Moreover, all
AONT-based techniques are unadapted for data streaming scenarios.

Second, the question of an efficient access management arises when data are
shared between several participants [2,6]. Especially, access revocation may be
problematic, as the data have to be re-encrypted with a fresh key (and this can
be realized only once the whole data are downloaded and decrypted at user's
device). A way of dealing with that issue consists in creating dependencies inside
encrypted data, so it is sufficient to just re-encrypt a part of data with a new key
in order to unable the access for a user in possession of the previous encryption
key [2]. Alike solutions protecting against key exposure, this requires additional
processing during encryption and does not fit data streaming use cases.

Here, we propose a Fast and Scalable Fragmentation Algorithm (FSFA), a
novel approach for data protection in an environment composed of several independent storage sites, that takes full advantage of the possibilities lying in data
fragmentation and dispersal. It transforms user's data into multiple interdependent fragments. Recovery of even the smallest part of a single fragment depends
on an equivalent size of content inside one or more different fragments. In addition, data are shredded before and permuted after the encoding to increase
the difficulty of data recovery from an incomplete set of data fragments. FSFA
achieves better performance than relevant techniques (including data encryption
and straightforward fragmentation) and does not make use of a key. It addresses
the needs of a user fearing about disclosure of their outsourced data, but desiring
the storage solution to be as fast, scalable, and inexpensive as possible.

An information dispersal scheme was sketched out in our short three pages
poster publication [12]. It has a limited domain of application, because its performance strongly depends on the chosen number of fragments. Here, we present
a thoroughly revisited version of this scheme addressing scalability and performance.

Outline. This paper is organized as follows. After describing relevant works in
Sect. 2, we detail our algorithm and its data model (Sects. 3 and 4). We compare it with state-of-the-art techniques in terms of security (Sect. 5), as well as
complexity and memory occupation (Sect. 6). In Sect. 7 we present performance
results. An insight into future works ends up the paper.

2   Related Works to Data Fragmentation

The following notations will be used during descriptions. d denotes initial data of size $|d|$ bits that is fragmented into n fragments, at least k (k is known in the literature as a threshold) of which are needed for data recovery. f denotes a data fragment of size $|f|$ bits coming from a fragmentation of d. The exact size of f depends on the applied fragmentation algorithm.

2.1   Multi-cloud Data Dispersal

Several authors already proposed to use not one but two or more independent storage providers to improve data confidentiality, availability or integrity [3,4]. Database solutions fragments data along their structure in order to break the dependencies [1,9], while object storage systems apply different fragmentation techniques from data shredding to perfect or computational secret sharing [3,5,8, 15,20]. The choice of the right fragmentation technique depends on the given use case, as it is usually a compromise between the desired level of data protection, the produced storage overhead, and the fragmentation performance.

2.2   Fragmentation Techniques

We selected four relevant works from the domain. Two of them are precise algorithm descriptions (Shamir's secret sharing and Rabin's information dispersal algorithm), while other two (Secret Sharing Made Short and AONT-RS) are flexible methods where one cryptographic mechanism can be replaced by another. A complete state of the art, showing that presented techniques had a vast impact and have been successfully transfered in the industry, can be found in [10].

Shamir's Secret Sharing (SSS): Shamir's secret sharing scheme [22] takes as input data d of size $|d|$ and fragments them into n fragments of size $|d|$ each, any k of these fragments are needed for the reconstruction of d. The scheme is based on the fact that given k unequal points $x_0, \ldots, x_{k-1}$ and k arbitrary values $y_0, \ldots, y_{k-1}$ there is at most one polynomial p of degree less or equal to $k-1$ such that $p(x_i) = y_i, i = 0, \ldots, k-1$. Data are transformed into n fragments $f_0 = (x_0, y_0), \ldots, f_{n-1} = (x_{n-1}, y_{n-1})$ that are points belonging to a random polynomial. Data d are encoded as the constant term of the polynomial p. The scheme provides information-theoretic security, but has quadratic complexity in function of k and leads to a n-fold increase in storage space.

Information Dispersal Algorithm (IDA): Rabin's information dispersal algorithm [18] divides data d of size $|d|$ into n fragments of size $\frac{|d|}{k}$ each, so that any k fragments suffice for reconstruction. More precisely, n data fragments are obtained by multiplying vectors of size k containing elements of initial data by a $k \times n$ nonsingular generator matrix. Recovery consists in multiplying any k of these fragments by the inverse of a $k \times k$ matrix built from k rows of the generator matrix received within the k fragments. Input data cannot be explicitly reconstructed from fewer than the k required fragments [16]. However, some information about the content of the initial data is leaked, as data patterns are preserved inside fragments when same matrix is reused to encode different data vectors. Even with this weakness, IDA is still being considered as one the techniques that could be applied in a multi-cloud environment [5].

Secret Sharing Made Short (SSMS): Krawczyk's Secret Sharing Made Short [14] is a computationally secure secret sharing scheme adapted for protection of larger data. Data d are encrypted using a symmetric encryption algorithm and fragmented using an IDA. Encryption key is split using a perfect secret sharing scheme (usually SSS) and dispersed within data fragments. In contrast to SSS, the storage overhead of SSMS does not depend on data size $|d|$, but is equal to the size of the key per data fragment. Performance of SSMS depends on implementation details of the data encryption and dispersal techniques. In modern implementations of SSMS, the IDA is usually replaced by systematic Reed-Solomon codes [3,19]. This improves the performance, but allows a partial decryption of compromised fragments in a situation of key exposure.

AONT-RS: Alike SSMS, the AONT-RS method [7,20] combines symmetric encryption with data dispersal. Data d are first encrypted. Encryption key is then exclusive-ored with the hash of the encrypted data (so it is unrecoverable in the absence of the complete ciphertext). In a next step, data are fragmented into k fragments and $n - k$ additional fragments are generated using systematic Reed-Solomon codes [19]. AONT-RS was inspired by the all-or-nothing transform (AONT) introduced by Rivest [21]. An AONT is a preprocessing step applied before actual encryption making decryption infeasible unless possessing the entire ciphertext. Input data are seen as a sequence of messages. These messages are encrypted with a random key that is then exclusive-ored with messages' hashes. The Rivest's AONT is slower than AONT-RS, as it requires two round of encryption (one during preprocessing and one during actual encryption). However, unlike AONT-RS, it protects data in a situation of key exposure.

Secure Fragmentation and Dispersal: Secure fragmentation and dispersal [11] may be applied over ciphertexts obtained with block ciphers with a mode of operation using chaining between blocks (like Cipher Block Chaining) in order to protect encrypted data against key leakage. This algorithm is composed of two steps. First step separates consecutive blocks of the ciphertext. Second step separates bits of blocks over final fragments. Fragments are stored over independent storage locations e.g. clouds. In consequence, an attacker present in a single storage location is unable to decrypt a single block of the ciphertext even if they possess the encryption key. Secure fragmentation and dispersal may be integrated within SSMS or AONT-RS in order to reinforce their protection level.

3   Data Concepts, Definitions, and Prerequisites

FSFA fragments some data d into k final fragments that are dispersed over c independent storage locations, e.g. non-colluding cloud providers or independent storage sites of a single provider. Fragmentation process is performed in two steps. First, data are separated into k initial fragments. Second, initial fragments are encoded. In this section we introduce few data concepts and definitions that may help the understanding of the algorithm. We also point out few prerequisites necessary for an optimal execution of the fragmentation.

3.1   Data Concepts

We introduce the following key data components with their size in number of bits and their dimensions in terms of number of elements of which they are directly composed (i.e., a structure s is $|s|$ bits long and composed of $\#s$ elements):

- **Sub-block** (sb): a sequence of size $|sb|$ bits.
- **(Input or Encoded) Block** (b): a sequence of bits of size $|b|$ composed of $\#b = \frac{|b|}{|sb|}$ sub-blocks; we refer to input block when it belongs to the original input data or to encoded block when it is a result of encoding.
- **Data** (d): an input data of size $|d|$ bits composed of $\#d = \frac{|d|}{|b|}$ data blocks
- **Permutation Array** (pa): an array of size $|pa|$ bits containing $\#b$ values: all natural numbers in range $[0, \ldots, \#b-1]$ appearing in a random order.
- **Initial Pseudo-Random Block (IPB):** pseudo-random block used as a first block of a fragment. It comes from the xor-split of a permutation array.
- **Fragment** (f): a fragment composed of $\#f = \frac{|f|}{|b|} = \frac{\#d}{k}$ input blocks at the beginning of the algorithm; then composed of the same number $\#f$ of encoded blocks plus one IPB at the end of the algorithm.

3.2   Prerequisites and Index Notations

Size of Data d: Number of blocks inside the data $\#d$ should be a multiple of the number of fragments k. This can be achieved using padding.

Number of Sub-block Inside a Block: When the number of sub-blocks inside a block $\#b$ is greater than the maximum value that can be encoded on $|sb|$ bits, the size of permutation arrays is greater than the block size. To minimize memory overhead, the maximum size of the block should not be greater than the maximum value that can be represented on $|sb|$ bits.

Parameters k and c: In order to facilitate computation, the number of fragments k should be chosen as a multiple of c.

Index Notations: A fragment is denoted by f_j where j is an integer in $[0, \ldots, k-1]$. A block inside a fragment f_j is denoted by b_i^j, where i is an integer in $[0, \ldots, \#f]$. A sub-block at the position v inside a block b_i^j is denoted by $b_i^j(v)$, where v is an integer in $[0, \ldots, \#b-1]$. A value at the position t inside a permutation array pa_r is denoted by $pa_r(t)$. An initial pseudo-random block is denoted as IPB and comes from the split of a permutation array. IPB_z coming from the split of a permutation array pa_r is denoted by $IPB_{r,z}$, where z is an integer in $[0, \ldots, c-1]$ such that $j \pmod c = z$. By convention, an $IPB_{r,z}$ is also the first block b_0^j of the fragment $j = r \times c + z$.

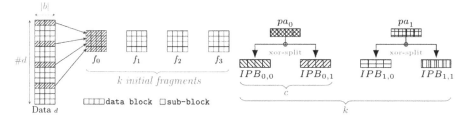

Fig. 1. Illustration for $c = 2$ and $k = 4$. **Left:** Dispersal of input data. Each fragment receives $\frac{1}{4}$ of the input data d. Any pair of adjacent blocks is distributed to different fragments. **Right:** Splitting $\frac{k}{c} = 2$ permutation arrays into k IPBs (each permutation array is split into c IPBs). As an example, $IPB_{1,0}$ will be appended to the fragment f_2.

3.3   Definitions

Our fragmentation algorithm creates dependencies between fragments at the level of data blocks and of sub-blocks using a modified version of Shamir's secret sharing. Dependencies are not equally strong between all the fragments, but each fragments is directly dependent only on $c - 1$ other fragments. To create such dependencies, each block of a fragment is encoded using $c - 1$ previously encoded blocks from $c - 1$ fragments. In order to facilitate the description of the algorithm we introduce the definitions of *neighbor fragments* and *parents blocks* defining data structures used during the encoding of a fragment and a block respectively.

Definition 1. Neighbor fragments. *A fragment f_j from the set of k fragments $f_0, \ldots, f_{k-1}$ possesses $c - 1$ neighbor fragments used during its encoding:*
$$f_{(j+1) \bmod k}, \cdots, f_{(j+c-1) \bmod k}$$

Definition 2. Parent blocks. *A block b_i^j belonging to a fragment f_j such that $i > 0$ possesses $c - 1$ parent blocks inside its neighbor fragments:*
$$b_{i-1}^{(j+1) \bmod k}, \cdots, b_{i-1}^{(j+c-1) \bmod k}$$

Dependencies between blocks are created in a chaining way, where an encoded block is re-used as a parent block during the encoding of the next block. First input blocks do not possess natural predecessors. Instead, initial pseudo-random blocks (IPBs) are used as their parent blocks.

4   Creating Fragments

This section details how data d are encoded into k fragments and how these k fragments are dispersed over c independent storage locations. A pseudo-code summarizing the encoding can be found in Fig. 2. The defragmentation process is not described as it is a direct inverse of the fragmentation.

```
1: function FRAGMENTDATA(d, c, k)
2:     f_0, ..., f_{k-1}=FORMFRAGMENTS(d, k)
3:     pa_0, ..., pa_{\frac{k}{c}-1} =GENERATEPERMUTATIONS(c, k, #b)

4:     b_0^0, ..., b_0^{k-1}=SPLITPERMUTATIONSINTOIPBS(pa_0, ..., pa_{\frac{k}{c}-1})

5:     while all #f blocks of each fragment are processed do
6:         for each block b_i^j of a fragment f_j do
7:             x=PICKEVALUATIONPOINT
8:             ParentBlocks =SELECTPARENTS(b_i^j)

9:             ENCODEANDPERMUTEBLOCK(ParentBlocks, pa_{j \mod \frac{k}{c}}, x, b_i^j)
```

Fig. 2. Pseudo-code of the function transforming input data d into a set of k fragments, that will be dispersed over k separate locations belonging to at least c independent storage sites.

4.1 Data Distribution over Fragments

In a first step, data $d = b_1, \ldots, b_{\#d}$ are distributed over k fragments $f_0, \ldots, f_{k-1}$ in such a way that b_i is assigned to $f_j \iff i \bmod k = j$ (FORMFRAGMENTS function). The number of blocks inside the data is a multiple of k, so each fragment receives exactly $\frac{|d|}{k}$ of the input data (illustrated in Fig. 1). This method of proceeding was chosen, as it allows to start the encoding of first distributed data blocks before the whole data are distributed over fragments in a pipelined manner. Data distribution over fragments could also be performed in a simpler way, by just dividing data into k consecutive chunks of size $\frac{|d|}{k}$ each.

4.2 Generating Permutations and Initial Pseudo-Random Blocks

Before the start of data encoding, permutation arrays have to be generated and split into initial pseudo-random blocks (IPBs). GENERATEPERMUTATIONS function generates $\frac{k}{c}$ random permutation arrays $pa_0, \ldots, pa_{\frac{k}{c}-1}$ of length $\#b$ containing all natural numbers from the range $[0, \ldots, \#b - 1]$ appearing in a pseudo-random order. The role of a permutation array is to mix up positions of sub-blocks after block encoding. This is done in order to slow down the recovery of relationships between encoded sub-blocks (see Sect. 5 for more explanation). We need multiple permutation arrays, as a fragment has to use a different permutation array than its neighbors.

Function SPLITPERMUTATIONSINTOIPBS xor-splits each permutation array into c IPBs (illustrated in Fig. 1). Obtained k (because $\frac{k}{c} \times c = k$) IPBs are distributed over k fragments in a way that IPB_{rz} is assigned to $f_j \iff r \times c + z = j$. $IPB_{r,z}$ becomes the first block b_0^j of a fragment j, when $j = r \times c + z$. Recovery of each permutation array requires all c corresponding IPBs. Therefore, we formulate the following dispersal recommendation:

Recommendation 1 (Dispersing IPBs). *Fragments containing IPBs allowing the recovery of a permutation array should be dispersed over independent storage locations.*

Remark 1 (Generating initial pseudo-random blocks (IPBs)). In order to minimize memory overhead, IPBs are used as shares allowing the recovery of permutation arrays at the same time being initial pseudo-random blocks used during the encoding of fragments. A different solution would consist in having both permutation shares and IPBs separated.

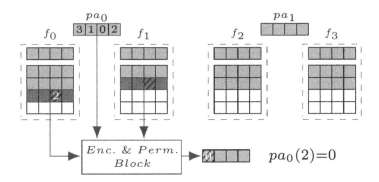

Fig. 3. Encoding fragments, example for $c = 2$ and $k = 4$. Fragments are encoded simultaneously, block by block. Input blocks (white) are encoded into encoded blocks (light grey). A current input block (dark grey) is encoded using $c - 1$ parent blocks (red) from its neighbor fragments. A current sub-block (dark grey, striped) is encoded using $c - 1$ sub-blocks from parent blocks (red, striped). After encoding, sub-blocks are permuted according to a given permutation. When $c = 2$, each fragment possesses one neighbor (as an example, f_1 is the neighbor of f_0). (Color figure online)

4.3 Fragments' Encoding

Encoding processing is sequential and performed on all fragments simultaneously, block by block (illustrated in Fig. 3). It creates dependencies between a fragment and its neighbors. More precisely, a block b_i^j inside a fragment f_j is encoded using $c - 1$ parent blocks from neighbor fragments of f_j. The processing is sequential and its philosophy could be roughly compared to the Cipher Block Chaining mode: once a block is encoded it becomes a parent block to another input block. First input block of each of the fragments does not posses natural parents (a similar problem occurs in CBC mode, where an initialization vector is introduced as the first block). Thus, for the k first blocks (IPBs) are used as parent blocks. As the are composed of pseudo-random values, they introduce pseudo-randomness to the fragments encoding. In order to increase the ratio of pseudo-randomness inside encoded data, fresh IPBs could be generated after encoding of a portion of input data.

Encoding and Permuting a Block. Input blocks are encoded and permuted inside the ENCODEANDPERMUTEBLOCK function (illustrated in Fig. 3, pseudo-code in Fig. 4) taking as input an input block b_i^j (where $j = 0, \ldots, k$ and $i = 1, \ldots, \#f$) to be encoded, its parent blocks, an evaluation point x, and the permutation array $pa_{j \bmod c}$ that will be used to permute sub-blocks of the block. Parent blocks are selected from neighbor fragments inside the SELECTPARENT-BLOCKS function according to the Definition 2. Parent blocks are the last $c - 1$ encoded (or permutation) blocks from neighbor fragments. The evaluation point x is selected inside the PICKEVALUATIONPOINT function. It is an integer in range of $[2, \ldots, 2^{|sb|-1}]$ ($2^{|sb|-1}$ being the maximum value that can be encoded on $|sb|$ bits). It is considered as a known value.

```
1: function ENCODEANDPERMUTEBLOCK(ParentBlocks,PermArray,x,b_i^j)
2:    for v = 0 : #b − 1 do
3:       a_0, ..., a_{c-2}=SELECTCOEFFICIENTS(ParentBlocks)
4:       b_i^j (v) = b_i^j (v) + xa_0 + ... + x^{c-1}a_{c-2}
    PERMUTESUBBLOCKS(PermArray, b_i^j)
```

Fig. 4. Pseudo-code of the function ENCODEANDPERMUTEBLOCK.

An input block is encoded sub-block by sub-block. The encoding procedure is based on a modification of Shamir's secret sharing. For each sub-block $b_i^j (v), v = 0, \ldots, \#b - 1$ an encoding polynomial is being constructed. $c - 1$ sub-blocks from parent blocks positioned at the same index v than the currently encoded sub-block are selected as the coefficients of this polynomial (function SELECT-COEFFICIENTS). The result of the evaluation of the polynomial at the evaluation point x is the encoded sub-block. In contrast to Shamir's scheme, the encoding polynomial is evaluated at only one point, as just one point in addition to $c - 1$ coefficients is sufficient for the decoding.

Intuitively, an encoded block and its parent blocks should be stored over separated locations, as reunited together they allow the decoding of the input block (in presence of the right permutation array). We formulate the following recommendation on blocks dispersal:

Recommendation 2 (Dispersing blocks). *A block and its $c - 1$ parent blocks should be dispersed over c independent storage locations.*

Encoded sub-blocks inside a block are permuted using one of the permutation arrays. An encoded sub-block $b_i^j (v)$ goes to position $w = PermArray (v)$. Permuting sub-blocks mixes up relationships between sub-blocks inside a block increasing the difficulty of data recovery from an incomplete set of fragments.

4.4 Dispersing Fragments over Independent Storage Locations

Fragmentation produces k final fragments $f_0, \ldots, f_{k-1}$ of size $\#f + 1$ each ($\#f$ input blocks and one IPB). Such final fragments should be dispersed over at least c independent storage sites, e.g. independent cloud providers. The dispersal procedure is defined a single rule: a fragment and its neighbor fragments cannot be stored at a single site. The total number of fragments k is the choice of the user: a higher value of k reinforces data protection against, as it allows to have multiple fragments dispersed over a single site. A weaker variation of the dispersal algorithm where only one storage location is used could be also considered: for instead to mislead a curious provider, a user can upload the data fragments from c different accounts. In the considered scenario, we assume that the user does not have to care about data availability or integrity, as they are usually guaranteed while signing the Service-Level Agreement.

5 Security Analysis

Each storage site receives $\frac{k}{c}$ non-neighbor fragments containing uniform and independent data (resistance to frequency analysis was confirmed by an extended empirical analysis not presented in this paper). An attacker situated in less than the totality of the sites can undertake two actions: to decode a portion of data from obtained fragments or to verify if data inside received fragments match some presumed data. To satisfy their curiosity, they have to overcome a combination of three obstacles: data fragmentation and dispersal, permuting, and encoding.

Data Dispersal. The first and simplest obstacle is the data dispersal. A single provider receives k fragments containing only a portion of encoded input data of size $\frac{|d|}{c}$ in total. Even decoded, information contained inside the fragments is sampled (result of FORMFRAGMENTS function) and incomplete. Moreover, if the cloud does not receive any information about the ordering of the fragments, there are $\left(\frac{k}{c}\right)!$ possibilities of fragments reassembling.

Data Encoding. Data encoding creates dependencies between blocks of fragments, as well as introduces pseudo-randomness to the data transformation thanks to IPBs. We formulate the following lemma, where by *infeasible* decoding we understand that for an encoded sub-block of size $|sb|$ an attacker must consider $2^{|sb|}$ possible values of the input sub-block:

Lemma 1 (Sub-block encoding). *Decoding of an encoded sub-block $b_i^j(v)$, $j = 0, \ldots, k$, $i = 1, \ldots, \#f$, without any knowledge about the input data and the $c - 1$ values of sub-blocks used during its encoding is infeasible.*

Proof. The procedure encoding sub-blocks of first input blocks applies directly the Shamir's secret sharing scheme, where $c - 1$ pseudo-random sub-blocks from IPBs are used as coefficients of encoding polynomials. Encoding results are outputs of an information-theoretically secure scheme, so they may be considered pseudo-random since we suppose that an adversary has no knowledge about the input data. They can be reused as encoding coefficients. The value of an encoded sub-block of size $|sb|$ depends on the $c - 1$ pseudo-random values of size $|sb|$. An adversary possessing an incomplete set of coefficients has $2^{|sb|}$ possibilities for each of the coefficients to consider. Depending on these coefficients, the input sub-block may take any of the $2^{|sb|}$ values.

Data Permuting. Permutations were introduced in order to protect against a powerful adversary that possessed a fragment and all but one of its neighbor fragments, as well as acquired partial or total knowledge about the input data to which the fragments belong. Such an attacker may undertake two actions: to recover the missing data part or to verify if the fragments correspond to the data. Without block permutations, they would be able to recover the first pseudo-random block of the missing fragments by reversing the encoding procedure. They can then proceed to the verification or to a partial data recovery. Permuting blocks increases the difficulty of reversing of the encoding procedure. Indeed, to recover values of a missing block an adversary has to check all the combinations of permutations of the sub-blocks. We formulate the following lemma:

Lemma 2 (Defragmentation of permuted data). *For an adversary possessing some knowledge about the input data contained inside a fragment, the difficulty of defragmentation or verification of a fragment without the presence of all of its neighbors increases with the number of sub-blocks inside a block and decreases with the knowledge of neighbor fragments.*

Proof. We consider first a situation where blocks are not permuted, but just encoded. For each encoded sub-block of a block it is possible to construct one polynomial equation of degree $c - 1$, where known or not sub-blocks from parent blocks are used as coefficients. Recursively, these coefficients may be also represented as polynomial equations, so at the end all sub-blocks may be represented in function of previously encoded sub-blocks, as well as of the first pseudo-random sub-blocks coming from IPBs. For a single block of $\#b$ sub-blocks we obtain then a system of $\#b$ equations. The difficulty of solving this system of equations depends on the amount of knowledge about input data and the amount of possessed IPBs. When data are permuted, $\#b!$ possible permutations exist, and as many equally probable systems of equations.

For a permutation array of size $\#b$, $\#b!$ possible permutations exist. If the blocks are composed of few sub-blocks, a brute-force search over all permutation possibilities is feasible. However, a $\#b = 34$ results in 2.95×10^{38} permutation array possibilities, which is comparable to the number of tries that are required to perform a brute-force attack on a 128-bit symmetric encryption key (2^{128} gives 3.4×10^{38} possibilities). An increase of the size of the block slightly affects the storage space, but also improves the performance of the fragmentation process (performance results presented in Sect. 7).

6   Complexity Analysis and Storage Requirements

Table 1 shows an overview of complexity considerations and storage requirements of concerned fragmentation schemes and of our proposal (FSFA). Algorithms can be divided into two groups. First group relies on symmetric encryption for data protection and combines it with a key hiding or dispersal method that prevents the key (and therefore the initial data) recovery until k fragments have been gathered. It includes all variations of the all-or-nothing-transform and Secret Sharing

Table 1. Runtime and storage requirements of relevant algorithms. $Poly\,(n,k,d)$: cost of encoding data d into n fragments using a polynomial of degree $k-1$. $Matrix\,(n,k,d)$: cost of multiplying data d by a dispersal matrix $matrix$ of dimension $n \times k$. $Encrypt\,(d)$: cost of using symmetric encryption. $Hash$: cost of data hashing. RS: cost of applying a Reed-Solomon error correction codes. $FragmentData\,(d,c,k)$: cost of data processing in FSFA. (d - initial data, $|d|$ - size of d, $|key|$ - symmetric key size, $|b|$ - block size in FSFA, $|matrix|$ - matrix in IDA, k - required number of fragments, n - total number of fragments)

Scheme	Runtime fragmentation	Runtime redundancy	Storage without red.	Storage with red.
SSS	Poly(n, k, d)	-	$k\|d\|$	$n\|d\|$
IDA	Matrix(n, k, d)	-	$\|d\|+\|matrix\|$	$\frac{n}{k}\|d\| + \|matrix\|$
SSMS	Encrypt(d) + Poly(n, k, key)	RS(n − k, k, d)	$\|d\| + k\|key\|$	$n\left(\frac{\|d\|}{k} + \|key\|\right)$
AONT-RS	Encrypt(d) + Hash(d)	RS(n − k, k, d)	$\|d\| + \|key\|$	$\frac{n}{k}(d + \|key\|)$
FSFA	FragmentData(d, c, k)	RS(n − k, k, d)	$\|d\| + k\|pa\|$	$\frac{n}{k}\left(\|d\| + k\|b\|\right)$

Made Short. Second group, comprising Shamir's secret sharing and information dispersal, encodes data using a system of equations, which is incomplete when less than $k-1$ fragments are present. Their big problem is the lack of scalability when the number of fragment k is growing, as a growing k entails a growing polynomial degree (SSS) or a growing dimension of the dispersal matrix (IDA). FSFA overcomes the scalability issue by introducing the c parameter. Data are dispersed over k fragments, but encoded using a polynomial of degree c. Following subsections give more details about the complexity and storage requirements of analyzed algorithms. Precise evaluation is hard because of the variety of implementations.

SSS and IDA: SSS computes n values of a polynomial $(Poly)$ for data d of size $|d|$. Its performance depends on the values of k, n, and $|d|$. Evaluating a polynomial is usually done using the Horner's scheme, which is a $O\,(k)$ operation. The cost of an IDA equals to the cost of multiplying data d by a $k \times n$ dispersal matrix $(Matrix)$. In both cases, data are usually first divided into smaller chunks and processed in a chunk by chunk fashion. They strongly benefit from an implementation in finite field arithmetic of the field $GF\left(2^8\right)$.

SSMS and AONT-RS: Performance of AONT-RS depends on the chosen encryption $(Encrypt)$ and hash $(Hash)$ algorithms, as well as on the data size and Reed-Solomon implementation. Wisely implemented, SSMS applies the same mechanisms than AONT-RS: symmetric encryption $(Encrypt)$ and Reed-Solomon (RS) codes for redundancy. Instead of hiding the key inside the hash of the whole data, SSMS disperses it within the fragments using Shamir's scheme

(*Poly*) applied only on the key. When SSMS is applied on data much larger than a symmetric key, the time taken by the key fragmentation is negligible.

FSFA: $FragmentData\,(d, c, k)$ is composed of several steps: generating and splitting permutations, data distribution, data encoding, and data permuting. The most consuming operation is the sub-blocks encoding. It takes $c - 1$ additions and $c - 1$ multiplications to encode a single sub-block, as the Horner's scheme for evaluating a polynomial is used. The procedure is repeated for all the sub-blocks inside the data, so at the end $\#d\#b\,(c - 1)$ additions and same number of multiplications are needed to encode the whole data. Because a $GF\,(2^8)$ finite field is used (like for SSS and IDA), a lookup table is used to replace the multiplications and the additions are replaced by exclusive-ors. Permuting sub-blocks may be implemented as a constant time operation. Data dispersal function FORMFRAGMENTS is an $O\,(k)$ operation. Being very simple and applied only once, data dispersal and permutations generation and splitting have a negligible effect on the algorithm performance. Additional fragments (if needed) are generated inside an optional procedure RS, which is exactly the same as the one used for SSMS and AONT-RS. FSFA produces $k|b|$ bits of storage overhead (k pseudo-random $IPBs$). A larger data block increases this overhead, but at the same time improves data protection and performance, as it allows a better parallelization of encoding. Defragmentation procedure is fully parallelizable, as a block may be decoded without waiting for decoding of predecessors.

7   Performance Evaluation

We benchmarked the proposed algorithm against the state-of-the art fragmentation techniques presented in Sect. 2. All schemes were implemented in JAVA using following resources: JDK 1.8 on DELL Latitude E6540, X64-based PC running on Intel® Core™ i7-4800MQ CPU @ 2.70 GHz with 8 GB RAM, under Windows 7. *javax.crypto* library was used to implement cryptographic mechanisms. Throughput was measured on random data samples of 100 MB.

Implementation Details. Similarly to SSS and IDA, the proposed algorithm can be implemented in any Galois Field $GF\,(2^Q)$. Q is usually selected according to the word size of processors and can be 8, 16, 32 or 64-bit. Presented version was implemented in $GF\,(2^8)$ enabling the use of only logical operations. Same field was used for the implementations of SSS and IDA. AES-128 in the CTR mode was used as the symmetric encryption algorithm inside AONT-RS and SSMS. AES-NI instruction set was enabled. SHA256 was used as the hash algorithm inside AONT-RS.

7.1   Comparison with Relevant Techniques

Performance of FSFA was measured for four different configurations: for two different values of c (2 and 3) and two different choices of block size (34, and 250 bytes: a block size of 34 bytes makes the recovery of a permutation array similar to performing a brute-force search on a 128-bits key, a block size of 250 optimizes the performance). Results are shown in Fig. 5. FSFA achieves much better performance than the state-of-art techniques. It is up to twice (for $c = 2$) faster than the fastest of the relevant works (SSMS with AES). As the cost of fragmentation and key splitting is negligible in SSMS, the performance of SSMS is equivalent to the performance of the algorithm used to encrypt the data. Thus, FSFA achieves better performance than data encryption with AES. AONT-RS is slower than SSMS (as hashing data is more costly than applying Shamir's scheme to split the key). In contrast to other algorithms, IDA and SSS do not scale with the number of fragments k.

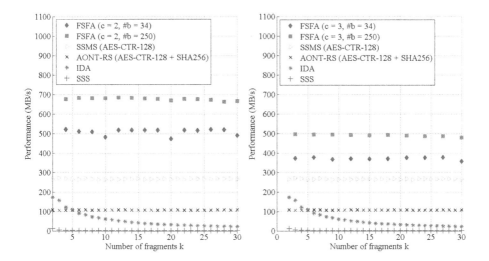

Fig. 5. Performance benchmark for $c = 2$ (left) and $c = 3$ (right).

Presented techniques were integrated within the DepSky multi-cloud environment [3]. Replacing symmetric encryption with FSFA resulted in a gain of $\tilde{2}0$–30% in performance on the client side. Results of an end-to-end performance comparison depend on multiple factors including the SLA and the data size.

8   Future Works

FSFA could be seen as a particular case of a more general method for data protection combining fragmentation, encryption, and data dispersal [17]. Modifications in the way of data dispersal over fragments, data encoding, or data permuting could be done (i.e., initial encoded blocks could be generated in a separated step, Shamir's secret sharing could be replaced with a different secret sharing scheme). From an implementation point of view, performance could be improved by fully exploiting various possibilities of parallelization of the processing.

In the future, the algorithm could be integrated inside systems that already use data fragmentation for other purposes in order to enrich them with an additional data protection mechanism. For instance, it could be integrated within the HAIL system that provides high-availability and integrity for cloud storage [4]. It could also be used as a fast way of creating dependencies between data in a fast access management system for outsourced data like the Mix&Slice [2].

9   Conclusion

A novel algorithm for data protection through fragmentation, encoding, and dispersal was introduced and analyzed. Data transformation into fragments relies on a combination of secret sharing and data permuting. It produces a small storage overhead proportional to the number of fragments, which is negligible in relation to larger data. Defragmentation of dispersed data requires the gathering of all fragments, which is possible only by acquiring locations and different access rights of several independent storage sites. Being keyless, the scheme may be used by a user fearing key exposure. Unlike variations of the all-or-nothing transform, the scheme is adapted for data streaming use cases. Performance benchmarks show that the scheme can be more than twice time faster than the state-of-the art comparable and widely renown techniques. The scheme is particularly well adapted for data dispersal in a multi-cloud environment, where non-colluding cloud providers ensure the physical separation between data fragments.

References

1. Aggarwal, G., et al.: Two can keep a secret: a distributed architecture for secure database services. In. Proceedings of the CIDR (2005)
2. Bacis, E., De Capitani di Vimercati, S., Foresti, S., Paraboschi, S., Rosa, M., Samarati, P.: Mix&Slice: efficient access revocation in the cloud. In: Proceedings of the 2016 ACM SIGSAC Conference on Computer and Communications Security, CCS 2016, pp. 217–228. ACM, New York (2016). https://doi.org/10.1145/2976749. 2978377
3. Bessani, A., Correia, M., Quaresma, B., André, F., Sousa, P.: DepSky: dependable and secure storage in a cloud-of-clouds. Trans. Storage **9**(4), 12:1–12:33 (2013). https://doi.org/10.1145/2535929
4. Bowers, K.D., Juels, A., Oprea, A.: HAIL: a high-availability and integrity layer for cloud storage. In: Proceedings of the 16th ACM Conference on Computer and Communications Security, CCS 2009, pp. 187–198. ACM, New York (2009). https:// doi.org/10.1145/1653662.1653686
5. Buchanan, W., Lanc, D., Ukwandu, E., Fan, L., Russell, G.: The future internet: a world of secret shares. Future Internet **7**(4), 445 (2015). https://doi.org/10.3390/ fi7040445
6. Castiglione, A., Santis, A.D., Masucci, B., Palmieri, F., Huang, X., Castiglione, A.: Supporting dynamic updates in storage clouds with the AKL–Taylor scheme. Inf. Sci. **387**, 56–74 (2017). https://doi.org/10.1016/j.ins.2016.08.093

7. Chen, L., Laing, T.M., Martin, K.M.: Revisiting and extending the AONT-RS scheme: a robust computationally secure secret sharing scheme. In: Joye, M., Nitaj, A. (eds.) AFRICACRYPT 2017. LNCS, vol. 10239, pp. 40–57. Springer, Cham (2017). https://doi.org/10.1007/978-3-319-57339-7_3

8. Cincilla, P., Boudguiga, A., Hadji, M., Kaiser, A.: Light Blind: why encrypt if you can share? In: 2015 12th International Joint Conference on e-Business and Telecommunications (ICETE), vol. 04, pp. 361–368, July 2015

9. Hudic, A., Islam, S., Kieseberg, P., Rennert, S., Weippl, E.R.: Data confidentiality using fragmentation in cloud computing. Int. J. Pervasive Comput. Commun. 9(1), 37–51 (2013). https://doi.org/10.1108/17427371311315743

10. Kapusta, K., Memmi, G.: Data protection by means of fragmentation in distributed storage systems. In: International Conference on Protocol Engineering (ICPE) and International Conference on New Technologies of Distributed Systems (NTDS), pp. 1–8, July 2015. https://doi.org/10.1109/NOTERE.2015.7293486

11. Kapusta, K., Memmi, G.: Enhancing data protection with a structure-wise fragmentation and dispersal of encrypted data. In: 17th International Joint Conference on Trust, Security and Privacy in Computing and Communications (IEEE Trust-Com), August 2018

12. Kapusta, K., Memmi, G., Noura, H.: POSTER: a keyless efficient algorithm for data protection by means of fragmentation. In: Proceedings of the 2016 ACM SIGSAC Conference on Computer and Communications Security, CCS 2016, pp. 1745–1747. ACM, New York (2016). https://doi.org/10.1145/2976749.2989043

13. Karame, G.O., Soriente, C., Lichota, K., Capkun, S.: Securing cloud data under key exposure. IEEE Trans. Cloud Comput. 1 (2017). https://doi.org/10.1109/TCC.2017.2670559

14. Krawczyk, H.: Secret sharing made short. In: Stinson, D.R. (ed.) CRYPTO 1993. LNCS, vol. 773, pp. 136–146. Springer, Heidelberg (1994). https://doi.org/10.1007/3-540-48329-2_12. http://dl.acm.org/citation.cfm?id=646758.705700

15. Li, M., Qin, C., Li, J., Lee, P.P.C.: CDStore: toward reliable, secure, and cost-efficient cloud storage via convergent dispersal. IEEE Internet Comput. 20(3), 45–53 (2016). https://doi.org/10.1109/MIC.2016.45

16. Li, M.: On the confidentiality of information dispersal algorithms and their erasure codes. CoRR abs/1206.4123 (2012). http://arxiv.org/abs/1206.4123

17. Memmi, G., Kapusta, K., Qiu, H.: Data protection: combining fragmentation, encryption, and dispersion. In: 2015 International Conference on Cyber Security of Smart Cities, Industrial Control System and Communications (SSIC), pp. 1–9, August 2015. https://doi.org/10.1109/SSIC.2015.7245680

18. Rabin, M.O.: Efficient dispersal of information for security, load balancing, and fault tolerance. J. ACM 36(2), 335–348 (1989). https://doi.org/10.1145/62044.62050

19. Reed, I.S., Solomon, G.: Polynomial codes over certain finite fields. J. Soc. Ind. Appl. Math. 8(2), 300–304 (1960). https://doi.org/10.1137/0108018

20. Resch, J.K., Plank, J.S.: AONT-RS: blending security and performance in dispersed storage systems. In: Proceedings of the 9th USENIX Conference on File and Stroage Technologies, FAST 2011, Berkeley, CA, USA, p. 14 (2011). http://dl.acm.org/citation.cfm?id=1960475.1960489

21. Rivest, R.L.: All-or-nothing encryption and the package transform. In: Biham, E. (ed.) FSE 1997. LNCS, vol. 1267, pp. 210–218. Springer, Heidelberg (1997). https://doi.org/10.1007/BFb0052348

22. Shamir, A.: How to share a secret. Commun. ACM 22(11), 612–613 (1979). https://doi.org/10.1145/359168.359176

Modelling and Risk Assessment

Cyber Insurance Against Electronic Payment Service Outages

A Document Study of Terms and Conditions from Electronic Payment Service Providers and Insurance Companies

Ulrik Franke[(✉)] [iD]

RISE SICS – Swedish Institute of Computer Science, SE-164 29 Kista, Sweden
ulrik.franke@ri.se

Abstract. Society is becoming increasingly dependent on IT services. One example is the dependence of retailers on electronic payment services. This article investigates the terms and conditions offered by three electronic payment service providers, finding that they only guarantee best effort availability. As potential mitigation, five cyber insurance policies are studied from the perspective of coverage of electronic payment service outages. It is concluded that cyber insurance does indeed give some protection, but that coverage differs between insurers and between different policy options offered. Thus, a retailer who wishes to purchase cyber insurance should take care to understand what is on offer and actively select appropriate coverage.

Keywords: Cyber insurance · Payment systems · Service outages
Document study

1 Introduction

In modern society, we are becoming increasingly dependent on IT services. IT brings value by enabling new services, or by making existing ones more efficient. The flip side of this coin is that the consequences of outages and disruptions to these IT services are becoming larger and more difficult to manage.

A relatively new tool for managing these increasing risks is cyber insurance. This tool, as an addition and a complement to the existing cyber security and risk management toolbox, has received much attention in recent years. For example, the EU Agency for Network and Information Security (ENISA) has published a number of reports on the effective use of cyber insurance [7,8], and the OECD is studying how to make better use of cyber insurance to tackle cyber risk management [16]. When the World Economic Forum presented a "playbook" for public-private collaboration to increase cyber resilience in January 2018, one of

© Springer Nature Switzerland AG 2018
S. K. Katsikas and C. Alcaraz (Eds.): STM 2018, LNCS 11091, pp. 73–84, 2018.
https://doi.org/10.1007/978-3-030-01141-3_5

the chapters was devoted to cyber insurance [21]. From the practitioner perspective, renowned IT strategy consultancies like Gartner offer advice on how to use cyber insurance effectively [20], and academically, literature reviews are being published [6, 15].

One example of a sector with growing dependence on IT services is the retail sector in its relation to electronic payment service providers. As put by Gartner, "payment functionality must be 24/7" [10]. In this respect, Sweden is an interesting example of a country at the forefront of the transition from cash to electronic payments. From its peak in 2007, the value of Swedish cash in circulation in 2017 has approximately halved [1]. The share of payments initiated electronically (measured by total transaction value) was at 98.3% in 2015 [2]. Even though at the moment, these trends are at odds with a global average where cash remains important [1], it is reasonable to assume that the future of payments is increasingly electronic, and studying an early adopter country thus makes sense.

Despite best efforts, in reality electronic payment services are not available 24/7. It is easy to find anecdotal media reports of outages in Sweden. In January 2018, payments could not be made with cards issued by the SEB bank for a few hours [19]. In July 2017, 13 000 point-of-sale (POS) terminals all over Sweden were unavailable for a few hours. The electronic payment service provider confirmed that the incident affected all sorts of businesses, and the spokesman is quoted as not being able to recall any outage of this magnitude having occurred before [18]. In August 2017, VISA card payments with some cards issued by the Nordea bank could not be processed [11]. The list goes on. Incidents like these are part of the motivation for the Swedish Civil Contingencies Agency in funding an ongoing research project addressing payment system resilience [12, 13].

Managing outages is one of the areas where cyber insurance can help. Whereas in the US, cyber insurance has traditionally mostly focused on 3rd party liabilities connected with data and privacy breaches, cyber insurance in Europe has to a larger extent addressed the 1st party costs of business interruption [9]. For example, insurer AIG reported in 2015 that while less than 20% of their cyber insurance customers in the US opt for network interruption coverage, more than 70% of customers in the EMEA region do [5].

The research presented in this article resides at the intersection of the two trends outlined above: (i) cyber insurance and (ii) electronic payment service resilience. More precisely, the research questions are: (i) What (basic) protection against electronic payment service outages is offered in electronic payment service provider terms and conditions, and (ii) what (additional) protection can cyber insurance offer? These questions are addressed through a document study of terms and conditions from electronic payment service providers and insurance companies active on the Swedish market.

The reminder of this article unfolds as follows. Section 2 briefly describes related work, situating the contribution within the existing literature. Section 3 then outlines the method used, before Sect. 4 describes the results. Findings are analyzed and discussed in Sect. 5, before Sect. 6 concludes the article.

2   Related Work

The literature on cyber insurance is relatively abundant. However, until recently, it has been characterized by a lack of empirical studies. In a now slightly dated literature review, Böhme & Schwartz note that the study of cyber insurance has been more concerned with developing theoretical models than with empirical research [4]. In a more recent review, Eling & Schnell conclude that more empirical research is needed, both on the demand and the supply sides [6].

Contents and coverage analysis of cyber insurance policies is an area where some empirical work has been done. A recent and relatively large-scale study was made by Romanosky et al. who analyzed more than 100 cyber insurance policies from the US [17]. The results give an interesting high-level view of cyber insurance, but do not answer specific questions about electronic payment service outages, and is limited to the US. Marotta et al. in their review catalog the coverage of 14 cyber insurance policies offered by the big global actors [15]. It is shown that they all offer some sort of business continuity coverage, but the details of this coverage with respect to, e.g., electronic payment services are not elaborated. Majuca et al. conducted an early study of coverage, which describes the development from hacker insurance policies in the late 1990 s to the more mature cyber insurance developed in the next decade [14]. However, this work is now more than a decade old, so it has limited value when assessing the current state of coverage. The same can be said of Baer et al. who show that business interruption was covered by all major insurance companies already in 2007, but gives no further details on electronic payment service outages [3].

To summarize, no existing work in the literature seems to offer a detailed analysis of how insurance policy coverage relates to terms of service offered in a concrete application domain such as electronic payment services. Thus, this article makes a contribution to the empirical cyber insurance literature, an area that has been identified as underdeveloped.

3   Method

The relevance of the research questions was first exploratively discussed with the Swedish Trade Federation. The Swedish Trade Federation also provided the terms and conditions of two major electronic payment service providers active on the Swedish market; Verifone and Nets. Verifone is one of the big global actors in payments services. In Sweden, they connect more than 26 million POS terminals to the cloud.[1] Nets is a regional actor in payments services, focusing on the Nordic and Baltic region, where more than 300 000 retailers used their services in 2016.[2] As these documents are also publicly available, these service providers are not anonymized.

---

[1] https://www.verifone.com/sv/se/om-verifone-sweden, accessed March 9, 2018.
[2] https://investor.nets.eu/nets-as-an-investment, accessed March 9, 2018.

As a complement to the traditional electronic payment service providers, the terms and conditions of challenger payments provider iZettle were also analyzed.[3] The iZettle Reader is plugged into a smart phone or tablet, creating a POS system that accepts not only (i) traditional card payments, but also (ii) contactless payments with cards or services like Apple Pay or Android Pay, and (iii) mobile payments such as the Swedish Swish service, which is based directly on bank accounts and circumvents the card infrastructure. Thus, even though when iZettle was founded in 2010, it built on the card system, it has now expanded into the cardless payments market. Arvidsson identifies iZettle as one of the causes behind the reduction in cash payments in Sweden [2], and this, together with its expansion into cardless payments, and its marketing tagline "never lose a sale" makes it a suitable complementary object of study.

Five cyber insurance policies were obtained from insurance companies active on the Swedish cyber insurance market as part of another study [9]. As these policy documents were obtained in confidence, and are not always publicly available, the insurance companies are anonymized throughout the study. More detailed anonymized information about the coverages they offer, their underwriting processes, and their typical annual premiums can be found in the previous study [9]. Additionally, non-binding recommendations by the German Insurance Association (Gesamtverband der Deutschen Versicherungswirtschaft, GDV) on general terms and conditions for cyber risk insurance were studied, as a sixth example of a cyber insurance policy. These recommendations are also publicly available.

All three sets of service provider terms and conditions were in Swedish, whereas four of the cyber insurance policies were in English with just a single Swedish language policy. The GDV recommendations were read in an English version, though the GDV makes it clear that this is for informational purposes only and that the German version shall prevail.

Regarding language and terminology, as pointed out by one of the reviewers, it would be good to be able to offer the reader a table of standard terms so as to better understand the contribution given in the next section. Unfortunately, there is no such standard terminology in place. Indeed, previous research shows that ambiguity about cyber insurance coverage is common [6,9] and the OECD identifies this as an important impediment on the demand-side of the cyber insurance market [16]. A noteworthy effort to rectify this is the work by ENISA to establish a common risk assessment language, resulting in a report published in late 2017 [8], but such work has not yet had any substantial impact.

The documents were read and analyzed with respect to the research questions, i.e. essentially from the perspective of a retailer who experiences an outage in the electronic payment service. Following preliminary analysis, some remaining questions were posed to the insurance company representatives. Most questions were thus resolved.

---

[3] https://www.izettle.com/se/pos, accessed March 13, 2018.

4 Results

4.1 Electronic Payment Service Provider Terms and Conditions

The *Verifone* terms and conditions[4] include several clauses that may be applicable to different kinds of service outages. While the service provider offers a support service where the physical POS terminal is replaced if broken, this service explicitly does not apply in case of communications network outages (7.1.b, 7.2). Service availability is explicitly addressed in Section 12 of the terms and conditions, where the service is described as normally being available 24 hours a day, but with exceptions for maintenance, upgrades, and planned service outages (12.1), which the provider reserves the right to perform as communicated on its website (12.2). In case of faults, outages, and disruptions, the provider is obliged to take action to restore service, but explicitly does not accept any liability. There are also some general clauses that may apply to service outages: Section 3.5. defines the service provided "as-is" with no guarantees made about its suitability for the customer or about continuous operation of either the POS terminal or the payment service. Section 22 limits the liability of the service provider to only direct damages to the customer caused by service provider violating the contract, explicitly excludes indirect damage such as lost revenue, profit or production (22.2), and also caps any liability accepted to the sum of payments made by the customer to the service provider in the six months before the incidents, though maximally three times the Price Basic Amount, an annually inflation adjusted sum currently 45 500 SEK (some €4 550). Finally, Section 23 is a *force majeure* clause, excluding liabilities for, e.g., power and telecommunications outages.

The *Nets* terms and conditions[5] are similar. Section 4 gives the service provider the right to interrupt the service in order to perform repairs, maintenance or improvements, or for other reasons, though planned service outages have to be communicated beforehand, if possible. It is also explicitly stated that the provider is not responsible for the availability or functionality of 3rd party services such as telecommunications or card acquisition (4). Section 7 defines the right of the service provider to discontinue service if the customer does not pay, and explicitly excludes any liability for resulting damages, including any lost transactions. Section 12 limits the liability of the service provider with regard to any specific indirect or additional damages to the customer, explicitly excluding lost revenue, profit, customers, and goodwill. Any liability for direct damages is capped to the sum of payments made by the customer to the service provider in the twelve months before the incidents. Section 13 is a *force majeure* clause, in general excluding any liability for damages resulting from the service provider not being able to fulfill the contract because of circumstances outside of the service provider's control. Section 13 also more specifically excludes liabilities

---

[4] https://www.verifone.com/sites/default/files/SE_Allmanna%20villkor%20tjanstepak et\%20v\%202016-11-01\%20.pdf, accessed March 6, 2018.

[5] https://www.nets.eu/globalassets/documents/sweden/in-swedish/terms-etc/nets_pa yment-terminals_terms_se_20170401.pdf, accessed March 6, 2018.

in certain jurisdictions for any damages caused by outages or lack of IT systems availability, as well as disruptions in electricity or telecommunications, and including computer viruses and data breaches.

The *iZettle* terms and conditions [6] follow the same pattern. Service availability is addressed in Section 11, where it is said that though service is normally available 24/7, the service provider does not guarantee that it is error-free or uninterrupted (11.1). Furthermore, it is explained that maintenance and upgrades can result in interruptions and that even though the service provider will try to communicate about any planned service outages beforehand, this is not guaranteed. The customer also explicitly agrees to understanding that "bugs" do occur, and can lead to disruptions (11.2). The service provider also explicitly excludes any responsibility for the availability of the telecommunications operator services that are needed for the payment service to work (11.3). Section 13.3 explicitly excludes any responsibility for the service being available at all times. Section 14.1 more generally excludes liability for indirect damages and lost profit, and Section 14.3 is a *force majeure* clause that also excludes any liability for the actions or omissions of 3rd parties.

4.2   Cyber Insurance Policy Coverage

On a very general level, typical cyber insurance policies can be described as composed of coverage of (i) 1st party costs (e.g., lost revenue from business interruption, cyber extortion costs, forensic and restoration costs, incident-related legal and PR costs, etc.) and (ii) 3rd party liability costs (e.g., notification costs related to data and privacy breaches, liabilities for spreading malware, fines, media liability, etc.) [9]. The policy parts investigated in this article pertain to 1st party costs, specifically the kinds of business interruption that can be caused by electronic payment service outages. In addition to the overall indemnity limit and deductible of the policy, business interruption coverage is also limited by a *waiting period*, which can be seen as a non-monetary deductible. Waiting periods may be as short as 6 or 8 hours, but are more typically 24, 36, 48, or 72 hours [9]. Only losses incurred after the waiting period has expired are covered. General exclusions common to all policies investigated include claims related to bodily injury and property damage, as well as *force majeure*. Specifically, the investigated policies can be characterized as follows:

Insurance company A offers coverage for business income loss (i.e., reduction in sales, etc.) and business income interruption costs (i.e., costs incurred to minimize the business income loss). The extent of the business income loss is determined using historical data pertaining to the insured's business before the incident, but the policy does not detail the calculation. Infrastructure failures, including electrical power interruptions and failures in telecommunications, are excluded, except for infrastructure that is under the control of the insured. Events at outsourced service providers are explicitly covered (with payment processing as an example). Depending on which additions are purchased, coverage

---

[6] https://www.izettle.com/se/villkor, accessed March 12, 2018.

can be either of only interruptions caused by security failures, i.e. antagonistic incidents, or of non-antagonistic systems failures, e.g., a patch that failed.

Insurance company B offers coverage for business interruption loss (i.e., reduction in net profit) and recovery costs (e.g., costs to remove malware, reconstruct data, find programming errors, etc.). The reduction in net profit is calculated based on the net profit of the period corresponding to the outage in the previous 12 months. Recovery costs are capped by the demonstrable business interruption loss. Both antagonistic (malware, hacking, DDoS, etc.) and non-antagonistic (human error, programming error, etc.) events are covered. Power failure is covered only in electrical systems controlled by the insured. A similar exclusion relates to outages in internet access, unless the infrastructure is under the control of the insured.

Insurance company C offers coverage for business interruption loss of profit and operational expenses (i.e., renting IT equipment and buying services to minimize the loss of profit). The loss of profit is calculated based on the profit earned in the previous 60 days, adjusted for a business trend. Notably, only antagonistic network compromise (e.g., unauthorized access and DDoS attacks) is covered. Electrical failure is excluded, except when caused solely by the negligence of the insured in performing technology services. Finally, the computer system affected must be controlled, operated or owned by the insured, creating something of a grey zone when it comes to electronic payment services.

Insurance company D offers basic coverage for business interruption loss. The loss is calculated based on the revenues earned in the past 36 months. In the standard policy, company D covers only this loss, but additional coverage for (i) mitigation costs and (ii) restoration costs is available as extensions. Mitigation costs are capped by the corresponding business interruption loss incurred. Similarly, only business interruptions due to cyber attacks are covered in the standard policy, but coverage of business interruptions due to (i) human error or technical failure as well as (ii) to legal or regulatory requirements are available as extensions. Business interruptions resulting from interruptions or disturbances in electricity, internet, telecommunications, etc. infrastructure that are outside the control of the insured are excluded, as are scheduled service interruptions (including maintenance or repairs lasting longer than expected) and any failure on the part of the insured to anticipate higher demand than normal. Finally, the standard policy limits coverage to insured's own computer system (which must be leased, operated or owned by the insured), so in order to cover an outage at the electronic payment service provider, an additional contingent business interruption (CBI) endorsement must be attached. This would essentially include the electronic payment service provider system into the definition and thus extend the cover to business interruption loss, but not cover any restoration costs for the service provider.

Insurance company E offers coverage for business interruption loss, as well as (i) forensic and restoration costs, and (ii) incident management costs related to insured incidents. The loss is calculated based on a reference time period three months before the incident, with room for additional adjustment. Outages in electricity, telecommunications, etc., are excluded, as are any losses caused by a business interruption being prolonged because the insured fails to follow instructions given, or cannot afford to take appropriate action. Antagonistic and non-antagonistic business interruptions are covered alike.

The insurance policy recommended by the *German Insurance Association (GDV)* covers business interruption loss (A4-1) as well as forensic cost and loss assessment expenses (A2-1). The interruption loss covered is based on a daily rate specified in the particular insurance policy (A4-1.3.1). Infrastructure outages such as interruptions in electricity, telephone, or internet service are excluded (A1-17.5), as are interruptions resulting from planned service outages, introduction of new software (including major releases of existing software used), untested software, or "software errors which are not based on a security gap" (A4-1.2). These provisions, in particular the last one, limit the extent to which non-antagonistic incidents are covered. Finally, losses resulting from the failure, interruption or malfunctioning of services from external service providers are excluded (A1-2.2), meaning that many outages in electronic payment services are not covered. In practice, the exclusion of external service providers may be carved back, but only restrictively and for named external service providers.

5   Analysis and Discussion

5.1   Protection Against Outages

The electronic payment service provider terms and conditions essentially guarantee best effort only. Though the service providers have some soft obligations to communicate about outages (planned and unplanned), all three sets of terms and conditions are explicitly excluding any liabilities for damages or lost income resulting from service disruptions. Liabilities for infrastructure outages in, e.g., electricity or telecommunications are also excluded. There are also some additional caps on any remaining liabilities. It is noteworthy that the terms and conditions of iZettle do not differ in any relevant way from the traditional service providers with respect to availability and liability for business interruption.

The insurance policies can offer some protection. While all policies offer some coverage of business interruption losses and costs to restore service, there are important differences: Some policies cover only antagonistic disruptions (e.g., DDoS or malware), whereas others cover non-antagonistic disruptions (e.g., misconfigurations or failed upgrades) as well. Some policies cover only interruptions in IT services directly controlled by the insured, whereas others cover interruptions in the external payment service provision as well. The principles for calculating the insured losses differ. Most insurers define a time period to be used as a reference, sometimes with provisions about additional adjustment, but the GDV recommendations instead suggest using a daily rate specified in the particular insurance policy. Finally, no insurer offers coverage of systemic infrastructure disruptions of electricity, telecommunications, etc.

To summarize, a retailer relying only on the electronic payment service provider terms and conditions will get best effort business continuity from the service provider. Cyber insurance can offer additional protection, in the form of risk transfer, for a wide range of business interruptions, but the details of the policy are important to scrutinize. Cyber insurance cannot offer protection against systemic infrastructure disruptions of electricity, telecommunications, etc. Such risks will have to be otherwise mitigated, e.g., using uninterruptible power supply solutions and standby generators etc., or just accepted. However, it is noteworthy that if a retailer does choose to invest in such backup electricity supply, and this also fails, many insurance policies *do* offer coverage of power failures in electrical systems controlled by the insured. Thus, such risk mitigation can also bring about some risk transfer, though the magnitude of such effort is probably prohibitive for many (smaller) retailers.

5.2   Validity and Reliability

Validity is very good, in the sense that the documents investigated are precisely the documents governing electronic payment service outages from the perspectives of the payment service providers and insurers, respectively. In the case of the electronic payment service providers, this is the case without exception. As for the insurers, policies are typically subject to some negotiation in the underwriting process, so the exact coverage can vary. However, negotiations mostly involves agreeing to which add-on coverage from an existing list is selected (well illustrated by Insurance company D above) and setting numbers such as waiting periods, deductibles, indemnity limits, and premiums. It is not the case that general exclusions applied by all insurers, such as the exclusions of systemic infrastructure disruptions, are in any meaningful way up for negotiation.

Reliability is also good. Though the documents studied are only samples from the larger sets of all electronic payment service provider terms and conditions and all cyber insurance policies, there are good reasons to believe that the samples are relevant and representative. In the case of the electronic payment service providers, the two traditional ones were chosen by the Swedish Trade Federation precisely because they are mainstream providers with substantial market shares. As for the challenger payments provider, the situation is more complicated, because on the fintech startup scene, there are many more upstarts than incumbents. The choice of iZettle is in this sense a compromise, selecting a major player with a substantial market share, but still a non-traditional company that has been instrumental in transforming the Swedish payment scene and now also works outside the card ecosystem. However, it is clear that the findings cannot be generalized to the terms and conditions of all upstart electronic payment service providers. In the case of the insurers, the sample covers about half of the market actors offering cyber insurance in Sweden [9]. Thus, it is known that the sample is not small and unrepresentative. Furthermore, the comparison to the GDV recommendations offers an additional perspective, indicating that the insurance policies on the Swedish market are quite similar to those (recommended) in Germany.

This leads naturally to the question of generalizing the results to other markets, beyond Sweden. Two strong arguments suggest that this is possible. First, electronic payment service providers are often global (e.g., Verifone) and terms and conditions are largely set by VISA and MasterCard in the form of the Payment Card Industry Data Security Standard (PCI DSS). As all electronic payment service providers need to adhere to this standard, the scope for deviation is small, and terms and conditions are very similar. Thus, the results of this study can reasonably be generalized to most countries.

A similar argument, though not quite as strong, holds for the insurance companies. None of the insurance companies investigated work in Sweden only, and most of them are global companies. Thus, much of the coverage they offer – and do not offer – can be expected to apply across many markets. Though offers can differ depending on regional demand as well as differences in law cross jurisdictions, the basic principles found in the insurance policy documents can be expected to hold in most countries. The most common difference is probably that cyber insurance is not offered at all, rather than that its coverage is radically different.

6   Conclusion

Uninterrupted access to electronic payment systems is becoming increasingly important to the retail industry. This has raised concerns, as electronic payment service providers only offer best effort availability (though it must be noted that this, for the most part, is very high). This finding is confirmed by the results.

One way to better manage the risk is to buy cyber insurance. The analysis in the preceding section shows that this is indeed a relevant tool, but that it comes with important caveats. A checklist for a retailer wishing to procure protection would include the following areas:

Non-antagonistic incidents are not always covered. The retailer should carefully consider whether such coverage is desirable, and if so, make sure to select an insurer offering it.

Systemic failures in electricity and other infrastructure is never covered. This risk thus has to be either accepted or mitigated with backup electricity supply, multiple telecommunications subscriptions, etc.

Interruptions in the external electronic payment service are often excluded from the policy as not being part of the insured's IT environment. Here care must be taken to re-negotiate policies, purchase add-ons, or switch to another insurer, to make sure that outages are covered. As some insurers require an ex ante list of the external service providers to be covered, care also has to be taken to understand the architecture of the card payment system, to get full protection.

The calculation of interruption loss differs between insurers, especially with regard to the time period used as reference period for the outage. Depending on the circumstances of the insured, some calculation principles may be more beneficial than others.

A few interesting avenues for future work suggest themselves. First, it would be interesting to complement the study by also looking at insurance claims, i.e., actual cases of electronic payment service outages being covered by insurance. This would require the cooperation of an insurer willing to share data, but would be rewarding in giving a more precise understanding of the coverage offered in practice. Second, it would be interesting to conduct interviews with retailers who have procured cyber insurance, or who have actively chosen not to, to learn more about how cyber insurance fits into their wider risk management strategies.

Acknowledgments. This research was supported by the the the Swedish Civil Contingencies Agency, MSB (agreement no. 2015-6986). The author would like to thank Bengt Nilervall of the Swedish Trade Federation for sharing electronic payment service provider terms and conditions, Dr. Oliver Lamberty of the Deutsche Rückversicherung AG for sharing the GDV recommendations and the insurance companies for sharing actual insurance policy documents and responding to some additional questions. Furthermore, the paper was improved by the comments of three anonymous reviewers.

References

1. Arvidsson, N.: The future of cash. In: Teigland, R., Siri, S., Larsson, A., Puertas, A.M., Bogusz, C.I. (eds.) The Rise and Development of FinTech: Accounts of Disruption from Sweden and Beyond, pp. 85–98. Routledge, Abingdon (2018)
2. Arvidsson, N.: The payment landscape in Sweden. In: Teigland, R., Siri, S., Larsson, A., Puertas, A.M., Bogusz, C.I. (eds.) The Rise and Development of FinTech: Accounts of Disruption from Sweden and Beyond, pp. 238–252. Routledge, Abingdon (2018)
3. Baer, W.S., Parkinson, A.: Cyberinsurance in IT security management. IEEE Secur. Priv. **5**(3), 50–56 (2007). https://doi.org/10.1109/MSP.2007.57
4. Böhme, R., Schwartz, G.: Modeling cyber-insurance: towards a unifying framework. In: Workshop on Economics of Information Security - WEIS (2010)
5. Camillo, M.: System failure: a real and present danger. Insurance Day (2015). https://www.aig.co.uk/content/dam/aig/emea/united-kingdom/documents/insurance-day-aig-cyber-article-system-failure-brochure.pdf. Accessed 9 Mar 2018
6. Eling, M., Schnell, W.: What do we know about cyber risk and cyber risk insurance? J. Risk Financ. **17**(5), 474–491 (2016). https://doi.org/10.1108/JRF-09-2016-0122
7. ENISA: Cyber insurance: recent advances, good practices and challenges. Technical report, European Union Agency for Network and Information Security (2016). https://doi.org/10.2824/065381
8. ENISA: Commonality of risk assessment language in cyber insurance. Technical report, European Union Agency for Network and Information Security (2017). https://doi.org/10.2824/691163
9. Franke, U.: The cyber insurance market in Sweden. Comput. Secur. **68**, 130–144 (2017). https://doi.org/10.1016/j.cose.2017.04.010
10. Gillespie, P.: The top 10 questions to ask when selecting a digital commerce payment vendor. Technical report, Gartner, Inc., October 2016, iD: G00311154
11. Tekniska problem för Nordea-kunder [Technical problems for Nordea customers]. Göteborgs-Posten, 25 August 2017

12. van Laere, J., et al.: Challenges for critical infrastructure resilience: cascading effects of payment system disruptions. In: 14th International Conference on Information Systems for Crisis Response and Management, pp. 281–292 (2017)
13. Larsson, A., Ibrahim, O.I.M., Olsson, L., van Laere, J.: Agent based simulation of a payment system for resilience assessments. In: Proceedings of the International Conference in Industrial Engineering and Engineering Management, pp. 314–318. IEEE (2017). https://doi.org/10.1109/IEEM.2017.8289903
14. Majuca, R.P., Yurcik, W., Kesan, J.P.: The evolution of cyberinsurance. arXiv preprint cs/0601020 (2006)
15. Marotta, A., Martinelli, F., Nanni, S., Orlando, A., Yautsiukhin, A.: Cyberinsurance survey. Comput. Sci. Rev. **24**, 35–61 (2017)
16. OECD: Enhancing the Role of Insurance in Cyber Risk Management (2017). https://doi.org/10.1787/9789264282148-en
17. Romanosky, S., Ablon, L., Kuehn, A., Jones, T.: Content analysis of cyber insurance policies: how do carriers write policies and price cyber risk? In: Proceedings of the 16th Workshop in the Economics of Information Security, WEIS 2017 (2017)
18. Tidningarnas Telegrambyrå: Problem med kortbetalning i hela landet [Card payment problems all over the country]. Sydöstran, 24 July 2017
19. Bankstrul för SEB - kortbetalning fungerar inte [Bank trouble for SEB - card payments do not work]. Värmlands Folkblad, 10 January 2018
20. Wheeler, J.A., Akshay, L., Proctor, P.E.: Understanding when and how to use cyberinsurance effectively. Technical report, Gartner, Inc., March 2015, g00274770
21. Cyber resilience playbook for public-private collaboration. Technical report, World Economic Forum (2018). http://www3.weforum.org/docs/WEF_Cyber_Resilience_Playbook.pdf. Accessed 9 Mar 2018. REF 110117

Semi-automatically Augmenting Attack Trees Using an Annotated Attack Tree Library

Ravi Jhawar[2], Karim Lounis[1], Sjouke Mauw[1,2], and Yunior Ramírez-Cruz[2(✉)]

[1] CSC, University of Luxembourg,
6, av. de la Fonte, 4364 Esch-sur-Alzette, Luxembourg
{karim.lounis,sjouke.mauw}@uni.lu
[2] SnT, University of Luxembourg,
6, av. de la Fonte, 4364 Esch-sur-Alzette, Luxembourg
{ravi.jhawar,yunior.ramirez}@uni.lu

Abstract. We present a method for assisting the semi-automatic creation of attack trees. Our method allows to explore a library of attack trees, select elements from this library that can be attached to an attack tree in construction, and determine how the attachment should be done. The process is supported by a predicate-based formal annotation of attack trees. To show the feasibility of our approach, we describe the process for automatically building a library of annotated attack trees from standard vulnerability descriptions in a publicly available online resource, using information extraction techniques. Then, we show how attack trees manually constructed from high level definitions of attack patterns can be augmented by attaching trees from this library.

Keywords: Attack trees · Semi-automatic construction
Information extraction

1 Introduction

Attack trees are a well known graphical security model [11,15,18–20], widely used in industry and academia for modelling threats and conducting risk assessment [22]. In an attack tree, the root represents the goal of an attacker, which is refined into subgoals, represented by its children, each of which may be in turn subdivided into subgoals, and so on. Originally, two types of refinements were considered: disjunctive refinements, which represent the existence of several alternative ways of achieving a (sub)goal; and conjunctive refinements, which represent the need of jointly achieving a set of subgoals. Extensions of this model include the definition of new types of refinements, such as sequential conjunctions [13,16,24] and parallel disjunctions [12], as well as the possibility to insert countermeasures into the tree structure [11].

S. K. Katsikas and C. Alcaraz (Eds.): STM 2018, LNCS 11091, pp. 85–101, 2018.
https://doi.org/10.1007/978-3-030-01141-3_6

Due to their graphical nature, attack trees are a convenient tool for the description and presentation of attack scenarios in an easy-to-understand manner. Additionally, they have been equipped with formalisms for conducting quantitative risk analysis [4,7,10]. However, the model has not seen a widespread adoption in real-world risk analysis settings. The major factor behind this problem is the set of challenges faced when creating attack trees. Two main approaches have been followed for creating attack trees. They differ from each other in the balance between human effort and automation. On the one hand, a completely manual process [4,22] is time- and labour-intensive, whereas on the other hand, completely automated approaches [5,8,9,17,23] tend to create trees that are too large, are hard to understand by humans, and have a hierarchical structure that does not fit the notion of refinement that analysts have, among other problems.

In this paper we explore one of the possible intermediate paths, where a part of the construction process is manually conducted by the experts and other parts are performed automatically. We view the construction of an attack tree as a semi-automatic process composed of the following steps:

1. A group of experts manually defines an initial version of the tree.
2. Some automated mechanism is used to enhance this tree using appropriate external resources.
3. The experts manually curate the new version of the tree.
4. Steps 2 and 3 are repeated until the final version of the tree is obtained.

The work presented in this paper focuses on the automatic component of this process, *i.e.* step number 2. Our goal is to provide a mechanism allowing the expert to profit from existing attack trees during the construction of a new one. To that end, we propose a method for augmenting an existing attack tree by attaching subtrees taken from a library, which is composed of existing attack trees. To support this process, we introduce an annotation of attack trees based on predicates representing the notions of assumptions and guarantees. This annotation is used to determine how the trees in the library can be attached to the tree in construction. The idea of formally annotating attack trees is not new. For example, Audinot et al. [1] use predicates representing pre-conditions and post-conditions on a state transition system to evaluate whether an attack tree is correct according to a system description. The purpose of our annotation is different. In our case, we do not have a system description, but a set of facts that are known to be true in the environment for which the tree is being constructed. More importantly, our annotation is not directly evaluated against a system model. Instead, we use it to decide whether, and how, a library tree can be used for augmenting the original attack tree.

Our Contributions. This paper presents the following main results:

– We define a predicate-based annotation scheme for attack trees that allows to determine whether, and how, an attack tree can be attached to another as a subtree.

- We propose a method for augmenting an annotated attack tree by attaching annotated subtrees from a library.
- We develop an instantiation of our approach, whose contributions are two-fold:
  - We describe the process of automatically creating a large library of structurally simple annotated attack trees from a publicly available resource, the National Vulnerability Database[1] (NVD).
  - We demonstrate the use of this library to augment annotated attack trees manually constructed from standard attack pattern specifications, thus linking two existing resources, the NVD and the Common Attack Pattern Enumeration and Classification[2] (CAPEC).

The remainder of this paper is structured as follows. Section 2 introduces the main concepts used throughout the paper, along with our annotation scheme for attack trees. Then, Sect. 3 is devoted to the description of our method for augmenting an attack tree with trees from a library. Finally, we present the aforementioned instantiation of our method in Sect. 4 and provide our conclusions in Sect. 5.

2 Annotated Attack Trees

We will first introduce the terminology and definitions used throughout the paper. An attack tree is a rooted tree that graphically describes an attack scenario. The root of an attack tree represents the global goal of the attacker and the children of every node represent a set of subgoals, referred to as *refinements*, of the (sub)goal represented by that node. Finally, leaf nodes represent *basic actions* that can be executed by the attacker.

Let $\mathbb{B}$ represent the set of basic actions and let the symbols $\bigtriangledown$ and $\bigtriangleup$ represent, respectively, disjunctive and conjunctive refinements. An attack tree is a closed term on the signature $\mathbb{B} \cup \{\bigtriangledown, \bigtriangleup\}$, generated by the grammar

$$t ::= b | \bigtriangledown(t, \ldots, t) | \bigtriangleup(t, \ldots, t) \tag{1}$$

where $b \in \mathbb{B}$. Figure 1 shows an example of an attack tree, which describes the CAPEC attack pattern 263, *Force Use of Corrupted File*[3], which describes an attack scenario where an application is forced to use a file that an attacker has corrupted, either by corrupting the sensitive file and waiting for the application to reload it, or by forcing the application to restart, thus reloading the file.

As we discussed previously, when manually constructing an attack tree, intuitive labels are often assigned to the nodes. While these labels may facilitate readability and visual analysis, they are informal, so it is not convenient to use them for automatically deciding whether a subgoal is susceptible of being

---

[1] https://nvd.nist.gov/General.
[2] https://capec.mitre.org/index.html.
[3] https://capec.mitre.org/data/definitions/263.html.

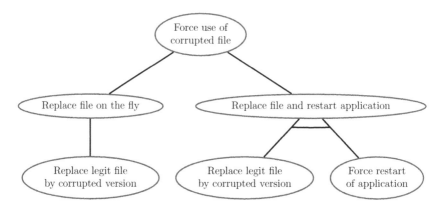

Fig. 1. An attack tree representing CAPEC attack pattern 263.

refined, discriminate between several plausible refinements, etc. [1,6]. To overcome this limitation, here we propose a formal annotation for the nodes of an attack tree. This annotation consists of pairs of predicates representing *assumptions* and *guarantees*. Assumptions encode properties assumed to hold in the contexts where the (sub)goal represented by each node is feasible, whereas guarantees are conditions that are ensured to hold if this (sub)goal is achieved. For example, in the tree shown in Fig. 1, consider the subgoal labelled as *Force restart of application*. Intuitive examples of assumptions that this subgoal may be labelled with are those describing the operating system on which the target application runs. Likewise, an example of a guarantee for that subgoal is that the application is writing its output to a specific directory. While these examples are useful for illustrative purposes, it is clear that the nature of the assumptions and guarantees to use for the annotation needs to be expressible in a language that allows for effectively automatic processing. Examples of such languages are decidable subsets of first order logic. In Sect. 4, we will discuss a particular implementation of our approach that uses Prolog facts, automatically generated from publicly available information sources, as assumptions and guarantees.

In what follows, we will first formalise the notion of annotated attack tree, and then we will discuss the notion of consistency, which will be used for characterising valid annotations of attack trees. The consistency of annotations will play a key role in determining whether, and how, an attack tree can be attached to another one.

Let $\mathcal{E}$ be a set of predicates, or facts, and as above let $\mathbb{B}$ represent the set of basic actions. Additionally, we will use the symbol $\bot$ to represent a contradiction. An *annotated attack tree* is defined by the grammar

$$t ::= (p, q, b) \mid (p, q, \triangledown(t, \ldots, t)) \mid (p, q, \triangle(t, \ldots, t)) \tag{2}$$

where $p, q \in \mathcal{E}$ and $b \in \mathbb{B}$. In what follows, we will denote by $\mathcal{T}$ the set of all annotated attack trees. We define the functions $\varphi \colon \mathcal{T} \to \mathcal{E}$ and $\psi \colon \mathcal{T} \to \mathcal{E}$, which yield the assumptions and guarantees, respectively, associated to the root of an annotated attack tree, that is $\varphi(t) = p$ and $\psi(t) = q$.

Now, let $\Gamma \subseteq \mathcal{E}$. We say that Γ is *consistent* if $\Gamma \nvdash \bot$, that is, no contradictions are inferable from Γ. The purpose of Γ is to encode known properties of the environment in which the attacks described by the attack tree may take place. For example, when describing attacks on a computer system, the predicates in Γ may encode knowledge about the hardware and software, such as the operating system in use, the libraries and applications that have been installed, etc. Now consider, for example, that according to Γ the operating system is UNIX, and we have an attack tree t that, according to the assumptions $\varphi(t)$, describes attacks that exploit a vulnerability in a Windows library. Arguably, t does not represent a viable attack in this setting. An analogous reasoning is also valid for the guarantees. We also deem reasonable to discard the possibility of refining some subgoal of a tree with subtrees labelled with contradictory assumptions. Taking back the previous example, if a subgoal specifies the assumption that the operating system is UNIX, it makes no sense refining it with subtrees labelled with the assumption that the operating system is Windows. Additionally, we argue that, in a disjunctive refinement, the guarantees of a node should be inferable, in the context of Γ, from those of each subgoal; whereas the guarantees of a conjunctively refined node should be inferable from those of its subgoals combined. Finally, the guarantees for the subgoals of a conjunctively refined subgoal must not be in contradiction. We formalise the rationales discussed above as follows.

Definition 1. *Let t be an annotated attack tree and let Γ be a set of facts. We say that the annotation of t is* consistent *with Γ, and write* $\mathtt{ConsAnnot}(t, \Gamma)$*, if the following conditions hold:*

$$\mathtt{ConsAnnot}((p, q, b), \Gamma) = \Gamma, p, q \nvdash \bot \qquad (3)$$

$$\mathtt{ConsAnnot}((p, q, \triangledown(t_1, \dots, t_n)), \Gamma) = \forall_{1 \leq i \leq n} [\Gamma, p, \varphi(t_i) \nvdash \bot] \wedge \qquad (4)$$
$$\wedge \; \forall_{1 \leq i \leq n} [\mathtt{ConsAnnot}(t_i, \Gamma)] \wedge$$
$$\wedge \; \forall_{1 \leq i \leq n} [\Gamma, \psi(t_i) \vdash q]$$

$$\mathtt{ConsAnnot}((p, q, \triangle(t_1, \dots, t_n)), \Gamma) = \Gamma, p, \varphi(t_1), \dots, \varphi(t_n) \nvdash \bot \wedge \qquad (5)$$
$$\wedge \; \forall_{1 \leq i \leq n} [\mathtt{ConsAnnot}(t_i, \Gamma)] \wedge$$
$$\wedge \; \Gamma, \psi(t_1), \dots, \psi(t_n) \nvdash \bot \wedge$$
$$\wedge \; \Gamma, \psi(t_1), \dots, \psi(t_n) \vdash q$$

This definition of consistency will play a central role in our method for augmenting an attack tree using trees from a library. As we will discuss in the following section, our method will receive as inputs consistently annotated attack trees, and it will ensure that the augmented tree obtained as output continues to be consistently annotated.

3 Using a Library of Annotated Attack Trees for Augmenting an Annotated Attack Tree

As we discussed in the introduction, we view the construction of an attack tree as a semi-automatic process composed of four steps, out of which we focus on the second one, namely the use of an automated mechanism to augment a manually produced and/or curated version of an annotated attack tree, with the aid of appropriate external resources. Let t represent the current version of the annotated attack tree in construction. As we discussed in the previous section, the annotation of t is consistent with a given set of facts Γ. We define a *library of consistently annotated attack trees* as a set

$$\mathcal{L} \subseteq \{t' : t' \in \mathcal{T} \wedge t' \neq t \wedge \mathtt{ConsAnnot}(t', \Gamma)\}. \tag{6}$$

In Sect. 4 we will describe in detail an example of how a large library of annotated attack trees can be constructed. Now, we will focus on describing how such a library can be used for augmenting an existing attack tree.

Given an annotated attack tree t an a library tree ℓ, the purpose of our method is to select a set of subtrees $s_1, s_2, \ldots, s_k$ in t, and add ℓ to the set of children of the roots of each s_i, thus obtaining a new tree t' identical to t, except for the fact that every (sub)goal represented by $s_1, s_2, \ldots, s_k$ contains ℓ as an additional subgoal. In these cases, we will say that ℓ has been *attached* to t as a subgoal of $s_1, s_2, \ldots, s_k$. For example, recall the attack tree depicted in Fig. 1. If the library contains an attack tree describing how to remotely restart an application and another one describing how to presentially access a system and restart an application, both library trees can be attached to t as a disjunctive refinement of the leaf node labelled as *Force restart of application*.

The proposed method deals with two types of decisions. First, determining the subtrees of t to which library trees may be attached, and second, determining which library trees can be attached to those subtrees without violating the consistency of the annotation of the resulting tree.

Regarding the first issue, we consider two cases in which a library tree can be attached to a subtree s of t. The first case is that of an internal node which is disjunctively refined. In this case, we will allow a library tree to be added as an *additional* child of s. Doing this can be interpreted as providing a new alternative for achieving the subgoal represented by s. The second case is that of leaf nodes. In this case, we will allow a library tree to be attached as a *singleton disjunctive* refinement, so additional library trees can be attached afterwards. We deem it unnecessary to add subtrees to conjunctively refined internal nodes. The reason for this is the following. If a (sub)tree s of t has the form $(p, q, \triangle(t_1, \ldots, t_k))$, then from the fact that its annotation is consistent with Γ we have that $\Gamma, \psi(t_1), \ldots, \psi(t_k) \vdash q$. That is, the current subtrees already ensure all expected guarantees, so adding a tree ℓ will be redundant.

The second type of restriction limits the choices of library trees that can be attached to t. We will require that the annotation of the new tree t' obtained from t by attaching some library tree ℓ continues to be consistent with Γ. In order to avoid evaluating the consistency predicate every time we need to assess whether a library tree can be attached to t, we introduce the auxiliary predicate $\texttt{Attachable}(\ell, s, \Gamma)$ for a subtree s of t and a library tree $\ell \in \mathcal{L}$:

$$\texttt{Attachable}(\ell, s, \Gamma) = [\Gamma, \varphi(s), \varphi(\ell) \not\vdash \bot] \wedge [\Gamma, \psi(\ell) \vdash \psi(s)] \tag{7}$$

The purpose of this predicate is to evaluate whether ℓ can be attached to t as part of a disjunctive refinement of s. As we will show next, if $\texttt{Attachable}(\ell, s, \Gamma)$ holds, then the tree obtained by attaching ℓ to t as a part of a disjunctive refinement of s continues to be consistently annotated with respect to Γ, which is the condition that we require.

Theorem 1. *Let* $t, t' \in \mathcal{T}$ *be two attack trees consistently annotated with respect to a set of facts* Γ *and let* s *be a subtree of* t *such that either* $s = (p, q, \triangledown(t_1, \ldots, t_k))$ *or* $s = (p, q, b)$. *Then, if* $\texttt{Attachable}(t', s, \Gamma)$ *holds, the annotation of the tree obtained from* t *by attaching* t' *as a subtree of* s *is also consistent with* Γ.

Proof. We first address the case where s is a disjunctively refined internal node of t. Let $s' = (p, q, \triangledown(t_1, \ldots, t_k, t_{k+1}))$, with $t_{k+1} = t'$, be the result of adding t' as a subtree of s in t; and let t'' be the annotated attack tree identical to t, except that s has been replaced by s'. From the consistency of the annotation of t, we have that

$$\forall_{1 \leq i \leq k} [\Gamma, p, \varphi(t_i) \not\vdash \bot] \wedge \forall_{1 \leq i \leq k} [\texttt{ConsAnnot}(t_i, \Gamma)] \wedge \forall_{1 \leq i \leq k} [\Gamma, \psi(t_i) \vdash q]. \tag{8}$$

Moreover, since we assume that $\texttt{Attachable}(t', s, \Gamma)$ holds, we have that

$$[\Gamma, p, \varphi(t_{k+1}) \not\vdash \bot] \wedge [\Gamma, \psi(t_{k+1}) \vdash q]. \tag{9}$$

Finally, according to the premises of the theorem, $\texttt{ConsAnnot}(t_{i+1}, \Gamma)$ holds, so we can conclude that

$$\forall_{1 \leq i \leq k+1} [\Gamma, p, \varphi(t_i) \not\vdash \bot] \wedge \forall_{1 \leq i \leq k+1} [\texttt{ConsAnnot}(t_i, \Gamma)] \wedge \forall_{1 \leq i \leq k+1} [\Gamma, \psi(t_i) \vdash q]. \tag{10}$$

Thus, $\texttt{ConsAnnot}(s', \Gamma)$ holds and, as a consequence, the new attack tree t'' is also consistently annotated with respect to Γ.

We now assume that s is a leaf node of t, and make $s' = (p, q, \triangledown(t'))$. Again, we have that $[\Gamma, p, \varphi(t') \not\vdash \bot] \wedge [\Gamma, \psi(t') \vdash q]$ (because $\texttt{Attachable}(t', s, \Gamma)$ holds) and $\texttt{ConsAnnot}(t', \Gamma)$ holds because of the premises of the theorem. Consequently, we have that

$$[\Gamma, p, \varphi(t') \not\vdash \bot] \wedge \texttt{ConsAnnot}(t', \Gamma) \wedge [\Gamma, \psi(t') \vdash q]$$

so $\texttt{ConsAnnot}(s', \Gamma)$ holds and, as a consequence, also does $\texttt{ConsAnnot}(t'', \Gamma)$. The proof is thus complete. $\qquad\square$

With the previous definitions and results in mind, we now specify our tree augmentation strategy.

Definition 2. *Let t and ℓ be two attack trees consistently annotated with respect to a set of facts Γ. We define the function $r : \mathcal{T} \times \mathcal{T} \to \mathcal{T}$ as follows:*

$$r((p,q,b),\ell) = \begin{cases} (p,q,\bigtriangledown(\ell)) \; if \; \texttt{Attachable}(\ell,(p,q,b),\Gamma) \\ (p,q,b) \qquad otherwise \end{cases} \tag{11}$$

$$r((p,q,\triangle(t_1,\ldots,t_n)),\ell) = (p,q,\triangle(r(t_1,\ell),\ldots,r(t_n,\ell))) \tag{12}$$

$r((p,q,\bigtriangledown(t_1,\ldots,t_n)),\ell)$

$$= \begin{cases} (p,q,\bigtriangledown(t_1,\ldots,t_n,\ell)) & if \; \forall_{1 \leq i \leq n}\; [r(t_i,\ell) = t_i] \; \wedge \\ & \wedge \; \texttt{Attachable}(\ell,(p,q,\bigtriangledown(t_1,\ldots,t_n)),\Gamma) \\ (p,q,\bigtriangledown(r(t_1,\ell),\ldots,r(t_n,\ell))) & otherwise \end{cases}$$
$$\tag{13}$$

For an annotated attack tree t and an annotated library tree ℓ, $r(t,\ell)$ yields an annotated attack tree which is identical to t, except that ℓ has been attached to zero or more of its subtrees. From the definition of $r(t,\ell)$, note that when ℓ is attachable to a disjunctively refined node and also to some other node(s) in one or several of its subtrees, we only attach ℓ to the subtree(s), as far from the root as possible. This is simply a design choice, aiming to prevent an excessive growth of t, and doing the opposite would not be incorrect in terms of the consistency of the annotation of the resulting tree.

The function $r(t,\ell)$ can be efficiently computed by doing a post-order traversal of the structure of t. The time complexity of this operation is linear with respect to the number of nodes in t. Note, however, that its actual running time depends on that of the evaluation of the $\texttt{Attachable}$ predicate, for which we will describe an efficient implementation in Sect. 4. As a final remark, note that the curator of the augmented tree may prefer to collapse singleton disjunctive refinements introduced by the our method, as this operation helps to reduce the size of the final tree. However, keeping the original tree as a subtree of the augmented one may be convenient in terms of readability, as we will see in the following section.

4   An Instantiation of the Proposed Method Using Publicly Available Resources

In order to showcase the viability and usefulness of the proposed method, we first describe the process by which we created an annotated attack tree library from a publicly available database of vulnerability descriptions. Then, we discuss a case-study where this library is used for augmenting manually constructed annotated attack trees that describe well-known high level attack patterns.

We created the library from a subset of the entries of the NVD (National Vulnerability Database). This database contains a standardised repository of vulnerability descriptions, as defined by the CVE (Common Vulnerability and Exposures) List[4], enriched with meta-data such as platform information, severity scores, etc. NVD is publicly available[5] and its contents are frequently updated.

---

[4] http://cve.mitre.org/cve/.

[5] Available in https://nvd.nist.gov/vuln/data-feed. The data feeds are available in JSON and XML formats. For this case-study, we used the JSON releases.

For our case-study, we used the releases of the database covering five years, from 2013 until the update corresponding to October 31st, 2017. This selection contains 39,995 CVE's. We filtered the initial set of CVE's to discard those whose descriptions fail to comply with syntactic patterns that facilitate reliable automatic processing (as will be described in the next subsection) and obtained a final collection of 23,473 CVE's. From each of those, we created an entry in the annotated attack tree library. These entries can be seen in two manners. On the one hand, we can interpret each entry as a single-node tree specifying the action *Exploit the vulnerability described by CVE-YYYY-XXXX*. On the other hand, we can assume that further refinements of this action exist (or can be manually specified if needed) since the meta-data associated to CVE's contain a number of links to websites, some of which provide actual refinements in the form of detailed instructions, source code, etc. For the sake of simplicity, since our focus in this paper lies on the mechanisms to match library trees to subgoals of the attack tree being constructed, in our case-study we populated the library with single-node trees, annotated with assumptions and guarantees automatically extracted from the CVE's descriptions and meta-data.

Once the library was constructed, we manually defined high-level annotated attack trees that describe attack patterns from the Common Attack Pattern Enumeration and Classification (CAPEC), and automatically obtained augmented versions by attaching trees from the library.

In this instantiation of our method, and for the case study, we used Prolog (specifically SWI-Prolog[6]) to encode the assumptions and guarantees in the library trees. We also implemented in Prolog the rules to evaluate the predicate `Attachable`. A pipeline of Python scripts[7], along with the Stanford CoreNLP toolkit [2,14], version 3.8.0[8], was used for the automatic library construction. Finally, the implementation of the function $r(t, \ell)$ was written in Python, and the freely available module PySWIP[9] was used to interact with the Prolog engine.

4.1 Automatic Library Construction

As we mentioned above, each tree in the library has the form $t_i = (p_i, q_i, b_i)$ and represents the action of exploiting a known vulnerability, as described by some CVE. We now discuss how the predicates for the assumptions p_i and the guarantees q_i are generated. The assumption predicates are a disjunction of facts of the form

$$\texttt{affectedPlatform}(\texttt{cve}, [\texttt{vendor}, \texttt{product}, \texttt{version}])$$
$$\texttt{affectedPlatform}(\texttt{cve}, [\texttt{vendor}, \texttt{product}])$$

---

[6] http://www.swi-prolog.org/.

[7] The code and resources developed for our implementation are available at https://github.com/yramirezc/lib-annotated-attack-trees.

[8] https://stanfordnlp.github.io/CoreNLP/history.html.

[9] https://github.com/yuce/pyswip.

extracted from the meta-data associated to the CVE, which uses the unambiguous Common Platform Enumeration[10] (CPE) naming scheme for systems, applications, libraries, etc. For example, the metadata of NVD entry CVE-2017-6191 states that it affects the platform described as

cpe : 2.3 : a : apng_dis_project : apng_dis : 2.8 : ∗ : ∗ : ∗ : ∗ : ∗ : ∗ : ∗.

From this metadata information, we generate the two following facts:

affectedPlatform(cve_2017_6191, [apng_dis_project, apng_dis, 2.8])
affectedPlatform(cve_2017_6191, [apng_dis_project, apng_dis]).

We now describe the generation of the guarantee predicates. Each guarantee is a conjunction of facts of the form

allowedAction(cve, [s, v, o])

where each triple [s, v, o] represents an action. In order to obtain these triples, we used simple, yet highly reliable information extraction techniques, based on analysing the dependency trees of those sentences in the CVE descriptions whose syntactic structure matches some well-defined patterns.

The *dependency tree* of a sentence is a directed rooted tree that hierarchally organises (a subset of the) words according to their roles in the syntactic structure of the sentence. The edges of the dependency tree are called *dependencies*, and are labelled with information about the syntactic relation between the corresponding words. As an example, consider the following sentence, which is the description of the previously mentioned CVE-2017-6191:

Buffer overflow in APNGDis 2.8 and below allows a remote attacker to execute arbitrary code via a crafted filename.

Figure 2 shows the dependency tree of this sentence.

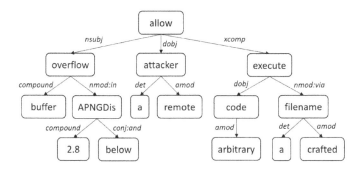

Fig. 2. Dependency tree of the description of CVE-2017-6191.

---

[10] https://nvd.nist.gov/Products/CPE.

Several tools are available for performing dependency analysis. As we mentioned above, in this case-study we used the dependency parser module of the well-known Stanford CoreNLP toolkit [2,14], version 3.8.0. The description of CVE-2017-6191 exemplifies the standardised language used in the subset of NVD entries that we selected for constructing the library. Even though these descriptions are given in natural language, they all contain at least one sentence whose dependency tree contains as a subtree one of the structures depicted in Fig. 3(a).

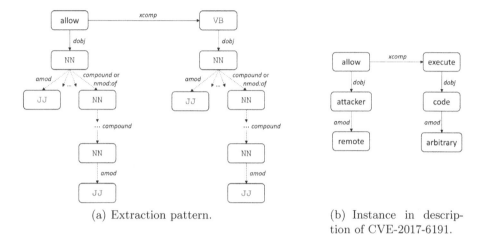

(a) Extraction pattern.

(b) Instance in description of CVE-2017-6191.

Fig. 3. Subtree-based extraction pattern used for obtaining guarantee predicates, and its instantiation in the description of CVE-2017-6191.

In the figure, solid arrows represent dependencies that must necessarily occur, whereas dashed arrows represent dependencies that may or may not occur. The labels NN, VB and JJ are the standard part-of-speech tags for nouns, verbs and adjectives, respectively; whereas the relevant dependency labels are *dobj*, *xcomp*, *amod*, *compound* and *nmod:of*. For a detailed description of the meaning of these labels and the linguistic foundation underlying them, we refer the reader to Appendix A and the works in [3,21]. In subtrees with this structure, the direct object complement of the main verb (*to allow*) is the subject of the action represented by the open clausal complement (*xcomp*). Considering this, for every substructure of this type that we found, we generated a fact of the form

$$\texttt{allowedAction}(\texttt{cve}, [[w_1, \ldots, w_t], \texttt{vb}, [w'_1, \ldots, w'_{t'}]]),$$

where $[w_1, \ldots, w_t]$ contains the set of nouns and adjectives in the subject of $\texttt{vb}$, whereas $[w'_1, \ldots, w'_{t'}]$ contains the set of nouns and adjectives in the direct object complement. Following standard practices in information extraction, in all cases we collapsed nouns, verbs and adjectives to their canonical forms, or *lemmas*. As an example of the fact extraction process, recall the dependency tree of the description of CVE-2017-6191, shown in Fig. 2. This tree contains as a subtree the structure depicted in Fig. 3(b), as a result of which we generate the fact

$$\texttt{allowedAction}(\texttt{cve\_2017\_6191}, [[\texttt{attacker}, \texttt{remote}], \texttt{execute}, [\texttt{code}, \texttt{arbitrary}]]).$$

4.2 Manual Annotation of Original Trees and Evaluation of the Attachable Predicate

We now describe the manual annotation of assumptions and guarantees that must be conducted on the original trees so they can be augmented with trees from the library. To label assumptions, we used facts of the form

$$\texttt{assumedPlatforms}([p_1, \dots, p_t]),$$

where each p_i is a (possibly partial) platform specification. For its part, to label guarantees we used facts of the form

$$\texttt{requiredActions}([[s_1, v_1, o_1], \dots, [s_t, v_t, o_t]]).$$

Aside from the manual annotation of any particular tree, we additionally specified a common set of Prolog rules for evaluating the predicate Attachable on any tree. By means of these rules, we make

$$\varGamma, \texttt{assumedPlatforms}([p_1, \dots, p_t]), \texttt{affectedPlatform}(\texttt{cve}, \texttt{p}) \vdash \bot$$

if p matches no p_i, $1 \leq i \leq t$. In this case, Attachable evaluates to false; otherwise, the result depends on the evaluation of the assumptions. By p *matching* p_i, we mean that p refers to the same vendor as p_i, as well as to the same product and version, if p_i specifies each of these pieces of information. If p_i only specifies partial information, e.g. vendor only, and it coincides with the equivalent pieces of information in p, then p is also considered to match p_i. For example, [cisco, residential_gateway_firmware] matches itself, as well as [cisco]. For experimental purposes, we additionally allow the assumptions label of some nodes of the tree to be one of the facts attachNothing, which always makes Attachable evaluate to false; and attachAnything, which makes the final result depend on the evaluation of the guarantees. Finally, according to the defined rules, we make

$$\varGamma, \texttt{allowedAction}(\texttt{cve}, [s_1, v_1, o_1]), \dots, \texttt{allowedAction}(\texttt{cve}, [s_t, v_t, o_t])$$
$$\vdash \texttt{requiredActions}([[s_1, v_1, o_1], \dots, [s_{t'}, v_{t'}, o_{t'}]])$$

if every required action $[s_i, v_i, o_i]$ matches an allowed action $[s_j, v_j, o_j]$. In this case, a match exists if v_i and v_j are identical, s_i and s_j satisfy set equality, and so do o_i and o_j. For example, the action [[remote, attacker], overwrite, [file]] matches [[attacker, remote], overwrite, [file]], but does not match [[attacker], overwrite, [file]]. For experimental purposes, we additionally allow the guarantees label of some nodes of the tree to be the fact everything Guaranteed, which makes the final result depend on the compliance of the library tree with the assumptions.

4.3 An Example of the Execution of Our Method

We now discuss in detail one example to show the characteristics of the augmented trees that can be obtained by our method. In order to manually create an initial attack tree, we selected from CAPEC the meta-attack pattern no. 165, *File Manipulation*, an instance of the category 262, *Manipulate System Resources*. Among the instances of this meta-attack pattern, we selected the attack pattern no. 263, *Force Use of Corrupted Files*, which has been discussed in previous sections (recall Fig. 1 for reference).

We created the following four different annotated versions of this tree, which differ from each other in the assumptions used for labelling the leaf nodes:

i. All leaf nodes are labelled with `attachAnything`.
ii. All leaf nodes are labelled with `assumedPlatforms([[cisco]])`.
iii. All leaf nodes are labelled with `assumedPlatforms([[theforeman, foreman]])`.
iv. All leaf nodes are labelled with `assumedPlatforms([[theforeman, foreman], [cisco]])`.

For all four annotation variants, we specified the same guarantee annotation. Recall from Fig. 1 that this attack tree has three leaf nodes, two of them labelled as *Replace legit file by corrupted version* and the other one labelled as *Force restart of application*. For simplicity, we will refer to the former two leaf nodes as b_1 and b_2, and to the latter as b_3. We labelled both b_1 and b_2 with the guarantee

$$\texttt{requiredActions([[[remote, attacker], overwrite, [arbitrary, file]]]}),$$

whereas b_3 was labelled with the guarantee

$$\texttt{requiredActions([[[remote, attacker], execute, [arbitrary, command]]]}).$$

Once the manual annotations were complete, we iteratively applied the function $r(t, \ell)$ on each annotated variant for every library tree. Table 1 summarises the number of library trees attached by applying the augmentation process to each annotated variant.

Table 1. Number of library trees attached to each annotated tree variant.

Variant	Attached to b_1	Attached to b_2	Attached to b_3	Total attached
i	10	10	182	202
ii	1	1	11	13
iii	1	1	2	4
iv	2	2	13	17

In every case, the leaves of the original annotated tree are now disjunctively refined with sets of library trees indicating which NVD vulnerabilities may be exploited to obtain the respective subgoals. As expected, for the first variant, which sets no *a priori* assumptions about the environment where the attack will be executed, the augmented tree is considerably large, which in turn makes it difficult to be read and used by human analysts. The remaining variants, by fine-tuning the platform-related assumptions, result in smaller augmented trees, which are not only easier to read and analyse by humans, but are arguably better suited to each specific scenario. To illustrate the output of our method, Fig. 4 shows the augmented tree obtained for the annotated variant *iii*.

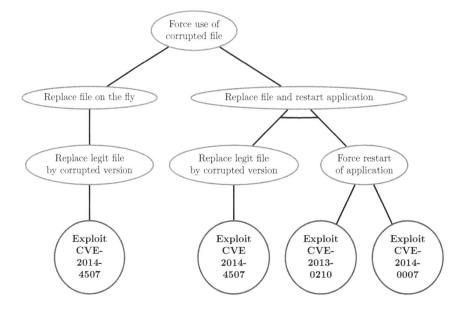

Fig. 4. Augmented tree obtained for the annotated variant *iii*.

5   Conclusions and Future Work

In this paper we have presented a method for assisting the semi-automatic creation of attack trees by augmenting an attack tree with subtrees from a library. The process is supported by an annotation of attack trees based on assumption and guarantee predicates. We have showcased the feasibility of our approach by automatically generating a library of attack trees from standardised vulnerability descriptions in the NVD, and using trees from this library to augment a manually constructed annotated attack tree representing a high level attack pattern described in CAPEC.

The results presented in this paper can be extended in several interesting ways. For example, similar approaches may be useful for automatically generating libraries of countermeasures, which can in turn be used to augment attack-defence trees or to convert an attack tree into an attack-defence tree by semi-automatically attaching countermeasures. Moreover, in the instantiation of our method presented in Sect. 4, we can move from the current static library to a dynamic one, by exploiting the syndication services provided by NVD, which allow to access new and updated CVEs when they are available. A dynamic library would in turn allow analysts to maintain dynamic attack trees, which is an interesting research subject on its own.

Acknowledgements. The research reported in this paper received funding from Luxembourg's Fonds National de la Recherche (FNR), under grant C13/IS/5809105 (ADT2P).

A   List of Dependency Labels Used in Section 4

These are the relevant dependency labels used in Subsect. 4.1 for the extraction patterns that enable the automatic generation of guarantee predicates for the library trees:

- *dobj*: main noun of the direct object complement.
- *xcomp*: main verb of an open clausal complement. This is the relation between the main verb of the sentence (*to allow* in the cases processed here) and the main verb of a subordinate sentence serving as clausal complement (in this case, the subordinate sentence describing the action that is allowed).
- *amod*: adjectival noun modifier. This is the relation between the main noun of a noun phrase and an adjective that qualifies it, e.g *remote* and *attacker* or *arbitrary* and *code*.
- *compound*: noun compound modifier. Similar to the previous one, but referred to a composition of nouns, one of which modifies the other, e.g. the relation between *service* and *denial* in the noun phrase *service denial*.
- *nmod:of*: head of prepositional noun modifier introduced by the preposition *of*. Similar to the previous one, but referred to the composition of a noun and a prepositional phrase that modifies it, e.g. the relation between *service* and *denial* in the noun phrase *denial of service*.

References

1. Audinot, M., Pinchinat, S., Kordy, B.: Is my attack tree correct? In: Foley, S.N., Gollmann, D., Snekkenes, E. (eds.) ESORICS 2017 Part I. LNCS, vol. 10492, pp. 83–102. Springer, Cham (2017). https://doi.org/10.1007/978-3-319-66402-6_7
2. Chen, D., Mannin, C.: A fast and accurate dependency parser using neural networks. In: Proceedings of the 2014 Conference on Empirical Methods in Natural Language Processing (EMNLP), pp. 740–750 (2014)
3. De Marneffe, M.C., Manning, C.D.: Stanford typed dependencies manual. Technical report, Stanford University (2008)
4. Fraile, M., Ford, M., Gadyatskaya, O., Kumar, R., Stoelinga, M., Trujillo-Rasua, R.: Using attack-defense trees to analyze threats and countermeasures in an ATM: a case study. In: Horkoff, J., Jeusfeld, M.A., Persson, A. (eds.) PoEM 2016. LNBIP, vol. 267, pp. 326–334. Springer, Cham (2016). https://doi.org/10.1007/978-3-319-48393-1_24

5. Gadyatskaya, O.: How to generate security cameras: towards defence generation for socio-technical systems. In: Mauw, S., Kordy, B., Jajodia, S. (eds.) GraMSec 2015. LNCS, vol. 9390, pp. 50–65. Springer, Cham (2016). https://doi.org/10.1007/978-3-319-29968-6_4

6. Gadyatskaya, O., Jhawar, R., Mauw, S., Trujillo-Rasua, R., Willemse, T.A.C.: Refinement-aware generation of attack trees. In: Livraga, G., Mitchell, C. (eds.) STM 2017. LNCS, vol. 10547, pp. 164–179. Springer, Cham (2017). https://doi.org/10.1007/978-3-319-68063-7_11

7. Hansen, R.R., Jensen, P.G., Larsen, K.G., Legay, A., Poulsen, D.B.: Quantitative evaluation of attack defense trees using stochastic timed automata. In: Liu, P., Mauw, S., Stølen, K. (eds.) GraMSec 2017. LNCS, vol. 10744, pp. 75–90. Springer, Cham (2018). https://doi.org/10.1007/978-3-319-74860-3_5

8. Hong, J.B., Kim, D.S., Takaoka, T.: Scalable attack representation model using logic reduction techniques. In: Proceedings of TrustCom. IEEE (2013)

9. Ivanova, M.G., Probst, C.W., Hansen, R.R., Kammüller, F.: Transforming graphical system models to graphical attack models. In: Mauw, S., Kordy, B., Jajodia, S. (eds.) GraMSec 2015. LNCS, vol. 9390, pp. 82–96. Springer, Cham (2016). https://doi.org/10.1007/978-3-319-29968-6_6

10. Jhawar, R., Lounis, K., Mauw, S.: A stochastic framework for quantitative analysis of attack-defense trees. In: Barthe, G., Markatos, E., Samarati, P. (eds.) STM 2016. LNCS, vol. 9871, pp. 138–153. Springer, Cham (2016). https://doi.org/10.1007/978-3-319-46598-2_10

11. Kordy, B., Mauw, S., Radomirović, S., Schweitzer, P.: Attack-defense trees. J. Log. Comput. **24**(1), 55–87 (2014). Oxford University Press

12. Lounis, K.: Stochastic-based semantics of attack-defense trees for security assessment. Electron. Notes Theor. Comput. Sci. **337**, 135–154 (2018)

13. Lu, W.P., Li, W.M.: Space based information system security risk evaluation based on improved attack trees. In: Proceedings of MINES 2011, pp. 480–483 (2011)

14. Manning, C.D., Surdeanu, M., Bauer, J., Finkel, J., Bethard, S.J., McClosky, D.: The stanford CoreNLP natural language processing toolkit. In: Association for Computational Linguistics (ACL) System Demonstrations, pp. 55–60 (2014)

15. Mauw, S., Oostdijk, M.: Foundations of attack trees. In: Won, D.H., Kim, S. (eds.) ICISC 2005. LNCS, vol. 3935, pp. 186–198. Springer, Heidelberg (2006). https://doi.org/10.1007/11734727_17

16. Piètre-Cambacédès. L., Bouissou, M.: Beyond attack trees: dynamic security modeling with Boolean logic driven markov processes (BDMP). In: Proceedings of EDCC 2010, Los Alamitos, CA, USA, pp. 199–208. IEEE Computer Society (2010)

17. Pinchinat, S., Acher, M., Vojtisek, D.: ATSyRa: an integrated environment for synthesizing attack trees. In: Mauw, S., Kordy, B., Jajodia, S. (eds.) GraMSec 2015. LNCS, vol. 9390, pp. 97–101. Springer, Cham (2016). https://doi.org/10.1007/978-3-319-29968-6_7

18. Roy, A., Kim, D.S., Trivedi, K.S.: Attack countermeasure trees (ACT): towards unifying the constructs of attack and defense trees. Secur. Commun. Netw. **5**(8), 929–943 (2012)

19. Schneier, B.: Attack trees: modeling security threats. Dr. Dobb's J. Softw. Tools **24**(12), 21–29 (1999)

20. Schneier, B.: Secrets and Lies: Digital Security in a Networked World. Wiley, Hoboken (2011)

21. Schuster, S., Manning, C.D.: Enhanced english universal dependencies: an improved representation for natural language understanding tasks. In: Proceedings of LREC 2016 (2016)

22. Shostack, A.: Threat modeling: Designing for security. Wiley, Hoboken (2014)
23. Vigo, R., Nielsen, F., Nielson, H.R.: Automated generation of attack trees. In: Proceedings of CSF 2014, pp. 337–350. IEEE (2014)
24. Jürgenson, A., Willemson, J.: Serial model for attack tree computations. In: Lee, D., Hong, S. (eds.) ICISC 2009. LNCS, vol. 5984, pp. 118–128. Springer, Heidelberg (2010). https://doi.org/10.1007/978-3-642-14423-3_9

Trust Computing

Tux: Trust Update on Linux Booting

Suhho Lee and Seehwan Yoo$^{(\boxtimes)}$

Dankook University, Seoul, South Korea
suhho1993@gmail.com, seehwan.yoo@dankook.ac.kr

Abstract. Preserving integrity is one of the essential requirements in trusted computing. However, When it comes to system update, even with the state-of-the-art integrity management system such as OpenCIT cannot properly manage integrity. This is because the updates are not transparent to the remote attestation server and the integrity value is not updated according to the updates.

This paper presents Trust Update on Linux booting, TUX. TUX collaboratively manages the integrity along with the kernel update, so that the update is transparent to the attestation server. With TUX, we can successfully maintain trust for the managed machines, even with frequent OS kernel updates. Also, TUX guarantees robust verified and measured boot to safeguard the integrity of a system's booting process.

Keywords: Open CIT · Intel TXT · Integrity · Security update
TPM · Trusted Computing Group · Grub · Shim · UEFI secure boot
Linux kernel

1 Introduction

As lethal security attacks, such as Spectre [5] and Meltdown [6], arise, the system administrators (admins) have been deploying security updates and patches continuously [8,10]. Considering the amount of efforts that have been putting into the security updates, the changing integrity of a system due to the updates has not drawn much attention. Maintaining integrity and applying security update share the same goal, securing the system; however, they take contradicting approaches. The former tries to prevent the system from unintended modifications, but the latter seeks to mitigate the vulnerabilities by modifying the system. This paradox makes guaranteeing the integrity challenging because the integrity is inevitably changed when the system update is conducted. Also, managing changed integrity can be frustrating when updates are frequent as is today.

Although several trust/integrity management schemes are presented [1,2,11, 15], these schemes cannot manage changing integrity according to the frequent updates. For example, Open CIT [11] implements remote attestation defined by TCG [13]. In Open CIT, the remote attestation server stores the whitelist value of its managed systems (clients) and validates the platform integrity based upon

© Springer Nature Switzerland AG 2018
S. K. Katsikas and C. Alcaraz (Eds.): STM 2018, LNCS 11091, pp. 105–121, 2018.
https://doi.org/10.1007/978-3-030-01141-3_7

the whitelist value. However, Open CIT fails to validate integrity whenever a client is updated. This is because the Open CIT server is not aware of the client's update state. Consequently, the server tries to validate the client with outdated integrity information and inevitably fails to attest the managed machine.

This paper presents Trust Update on Linux booting (TUX), a novel integrity management scheme which can adequately manage the integrity of Linux booting along with frequent updates. First of all, TUX makes kernel update transparent to the attestation server by integrating the update server to the Open CIT. Thus, Open CIT can manage kernel updates for each client, and Open CIT is fully aware of the updates of its clients. Also, TUX allows Open CIT to maintain up-to-date whitelist values; thereby TUX eliminates attestation failures caused by the unnoticed updates.

Secondly, TUX provides a robust verified boot which can verify the integrity of entire booting process using the TUX-secure boot (TS-Boot). TS-Boot is a combination of the UEFI secure boot, Shim bootloader, and Grub bootloader. Using the TS-Boot, TUX supports integrity verification using firmware key and TPM. The core idea is to measure entire booting process using TPM and compare it with known-good integrity value using the secure boot to check whether if the booting process has maintained its integrity. TUX will immediately halt the booting when the two values (TPM measurements and the known-good integrity) do not match. Additionally, this allows the distributors to manage client's booting policy, and restrict the attacks from compromised booting process.

The key contributions of this work are:

- TUX extends Intel Open CIT enabling integrity management under frequent updates.
- TUX hardens Linux booting by consolidating secure boot and measured boot.

This paper consists of the following sections. Section 2 provides background knowledge of contemporary integrity management schemes. Section 3 presents some threat models. Section 4 illustrates the design considerations of TUX. Section 5 describes some implementation issues in TUX. Section 6 evaluates TUX. Section 7 discusses further considerations not covered in this paper. Finally, we conclude the paper in Sect. 8.

2 Background

2.1 TPM

Trusted Platform Module (TPM) [14] is an independent hardware which is designed to measure integrity safely. TPM was proposed by the Trusted Computing Group (TCG) [13] to provide a trusted execution environment that can measure and store the integrity. TPM measures platform integrity with its cryptography processor and stores it to the Platform Configuration Registers (PCRs). PCRs are tamper proof registers that stores integrity hash values. Also, TPM creates chain-of-trust with *extend* operation, which allows TPM to calculate new integrity value from the old value.

2.2   tboot and LCP

Trusted Boot (tboot) [16] is a bootloader module which adopts Intel Trust Execution Technology (TXT) [2] to support measured and verified boot. Using the TXT, tboot measures platform's pre-boot environment from the hardware initialization to the loaded kernel binary. Also, tboot verifies platform integrity with the Launch Control Policy (LCP), a pre-defined list of known-good values of allowed properties. LCP defines integrity of the BIOS configurations, bootloader, OS kernel, and LCP itself with its three policies: SINIT, Platform configuration (PCONF), and Measured Launch Environment (MLE). tboot verifies the integrity by comparing TPM measurements against the LCP and states the booting is trusted when all three policies are met.

Although the tboot guarantees the robust integrity of the pre-boot environment, it can be restricted when frequent updates are conducted. The LCP is bound to a specific state of the platform, and thus, when the platform is updated, the LCP also needs to be updated according to up-to-date status. LCP update regarding a small number of devices may be manageable, but the difficulty of management will increase exponentially as the number of devices to manage and issued updates increase. Therefore, tboot is not suitable for an environment with frequent updates. Additionally, tboot works as a bootloader module, making it vulnerable to rootkit attacks [3].

2.3   UEFI Secure Boot

UEFI secure boot [15] is a security standard defined in the UEFI BIOS. The secure boot enables robust firmware level verified booting by employing asymmetric-key cryptography. Secure boot mandates every booting component, such as bootloaders and OS kernels, are digitally signed with the distributor's private key. At the boot time, the UEFI secure boot verifies the signatures of the binaries using the distributor's public key stored in the firmware's db. when the binary's signature is verified, secure boot confirms the integrity of the file and executes the binary.

For Linux to support UEFI secure boot, it needs to use a first-stage bootloader, Shim [9]. This is because Grub, a bootloader to load Linux kernel, is not supported by the UEFI secure boot. Therefore, at booting, secure boot loads the Shim first, then Shim loads Grub bootloader. Also, Shim is capable of binary verification with the firmware key using the shim_lock verification.

Adopting UEFI secure boot can result in several advantages. First, it is supported by most of the platforms. Second, secure boot provides simple update procedure for the clients, compared to the Intel TXT. When a component is updated, the distributor only needs to sign the updated file with the private key and deploy it. Also, the client only needs to update the binary, no LCP update required.

However, UEFI secure boot is not satisfactory to guarantee thorough trusted booting. This is because the current secure boot does not provide integrity verification for some vital booting components, such as the kernel booting parameters, Grub commands, and Grub configuration files. Also, it does not support measured environment for the remote attestation.

2.4   Trusted Grub

Trusted Grub [1] is a bootloader for Linux that supports measured launch. Trusted Grub adopts TPM to establish the chain-of-trust of the booting stages. Trusted Grub measures thorough booting process by measuring not only the kernel binaries, but also the Grub configuration files, and loadable Grub modules.

Unfortunately, the official Trusted Grub only supports TPM v1.2. Note that the TPM v1.2 only support SHA-1 hash algorithm, which is vulnerable to hash collision attacks [12] and deprecated. Furthermore, Trusted Grub only performs measurements and leaves verification up to the remote attestation. Thus, it cannot guarantee the integrity of the platform on run-time as Intel TXT or UEFI secure boot.

2.5   Open CIT and Remote Attestation

Intel Open Cloud Integrity Technology (CIT) [11] is an Intel's implementation of TCG's remote attestation. Open CIT claims the integrity of the platform by verifying the TPM measurements measured using the Intel TXT. Also, Open CIT uses a unique application called *Trust Agent* to enable remote attestation. Trust Agent resides on the managed machines, and it implements *quote operation* to pass on the TPM measurements to the attestation server for verification. Also, it provides web-based monitoring tool, which allows users to initiate and manage remote attestation efficiently.

The remote attestation begins with the machine registration to the remote attestation server. At the registration, the attestation server imports measured values as the initial known-good values (whitelist) from each machine. Then, the imported values become the comparison basis to check the machines' integrity. After the registration, the server can perform remote attestation by requesting TPM measurements from the local hosts. When the Trust Agent receives the request, it uses quote operation to pass on the measurements. Then, received measurements are compared against the whitelist to verify the integrity. If the values do not match, Open CIT states broken integrity.

However, Open CIT has some limitation when it comes to an environment with frequent updates. This is because the update status of the clients are not transparent to the attestation server and the Open CIT can establish whitelist only by importing. Namely, when the update is conducted on the client side, the Open CIT encounters broken integrity since it does not have information about the update. Also, for every update, the attestation server must re-import updated values to re-establish comparison basis. This can be a considerable overhead for the Open CIT when updates are frequently conducted.

3   Threat Model

3.1   Subverting Open CIT

We assume that the adversary can update OS kernel and perform measured boot. In this case, the adversary can thwart remote attestation with the following scenario. First, the adversary updates the victim with a compromised kernel such as old kernel that includes known vulnerabilities. After the reboot, the TPM measurements are also compromised since it measures compromised kernel. Then, since the update was conducted, victim admin tries to import new measurements to the Open CIT server to re-establish the comparison basis. Note that Open CIT has no means to distinguish between legitimate updates from malicious updates. Therefore, Open CIT administrator, unfortunately, has no way but to import new measurement values to the server. Now Open CIT has compromised whitelist, and the remote attestation is performed using the compromised whitelist values. Therefore, the adversary can run malicious kernel even though the Open CIT confirms that the system is trusted.

3.2   Circumventing Verified Boot

The pre-boot environment can be a security hole [4], and this can be mitigated by verified boots, such as tboot and UEFI secure boot. However, [3] describes an attack that can undermine tboot using a thin layer of virtual TPM. Also, it is possible to modify the booting process using the Grub command line even though the UEFI secure boot is on. Both limitations are because they do not validate the executed Grub commands and modules. Thus, an adversary, who has physical access to Grub, can compromise Grub commands to run malicious modules, breaking the integrity in Linux booting process.

4   Design of TUX

In this section, we present the design of TUX, Trust Update on Linux booting. TUX suggests novel integrity management scheme, which can maintain thorough integrity verification along with frequent updates. TUX extends the Intel Open CIT by taking advantage of its robust attestation scheme and consolidating it with kernel update and whitelist management.

Assumptions. Before diving into TUX design, there are several assumptions to be considered. First, the attestation server owner, also known as the *TUX owner*, is considered as the administrator for update and management. Second, TUX verifies the integrity of Linux booting process only. This is because we believe that booting process is essential to establish the trusted environment and after boot environment can be handled with operating system's powerful security solutions. Third, TUX assumes that the attestation server and its components are trustworthy and secure. Fourth, TUX assumes that the TUX owner holds manifest of the entire booting process of each managed machine. Booting process includes all the hardware configurations, loaded software, executed Grub commands, etc. IT department usually manages hardware information of every computer because they are assets of an organization, and thus, it is reasonable to assume that the owner knows the hardware configurations of the managed machines. Finally, we assume that all of the managed machines have TUX owner's public key pre-installed.

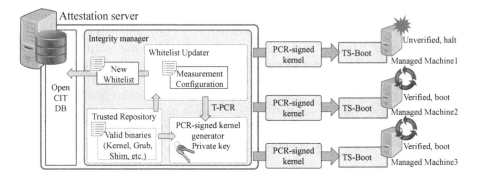

Fig. 1. The design of TUX

Figure 1 illustrates the design of TUX. As shown in the figure, TUX consists of three components: Integrity manager, PCR-signed kernel, and TUX-Secure boot. First, The TUX Integrity manager resides in Open CIT's remote attestation server to manage integrity along with updates. The TUX Integrity manager is composed of the Trusted repository, Whitelist updater, and PCR-signed kernel generator. Second, the PCR-signed kernel is a unique kernel that is deployed from the attestation server, which holds known-good integrity value inside its signature. Lastly, The TUX-Secure boot (TS-boot) is located at the managed machine. TS-boot provides solid chain-of-trust and integrity verification by consolidating UEFI Secure boot, Shim, and Grub. By using the PCR-signed kernel, TS-boot can verify entire booting process without LCP.

4.1   TUX Components

Here, we describe the three major components of TUX: Integrity manager, PCR-signed kernel, and TS-Boot.

Integrity Manager. TUX presents Integrity manager, robust integrity management and kernel update component integrated to Intel Open CIT's attestation server. With the integrity manager, Open CIT server transparently updates the managed machines and prevent un-intended attestation failure due to the updates. The Integrity manager focuses on whitelist value management and the PCR-signed kernel generation for integrity value deployment. As shown in Fig. 1,

Tux Integrity manager is consisted of three units to manage integrity: Trusted repository, Whitelist updater, and PCR-signed kernel generator.

Trusted repository is an update repository, which stores TUX owner's private key and valid kernel and bootloader binaries that are not stated as End-Of-Life (EOL). Binaries stored in the Trusted repository are under the control of TUX owner, allowing the TUX owner to take full control of the software used on the managed machines. Also, TUX Trusted repository provides the binaries to Whitelist updater and PCR-signed kernel generator for integrity management and deployment. Note that the attestation server is assumed to be secure; hence, the files in the trusted repository are also safe and trusted.

Whitelist updater calculates and updates per-machine integrity values within the attestation server. Firstly, the Whitelist updater dynamically calculates whitelist values and the Trusted PCR value (t-PCR) according to the Measurement configuration and the binaries stored in the trusted repository. Measurement configuration is a manifest of instruction sequence resembling the entire booting process, and the t-PCR is a known-good integrity value calculated by extending entire booting process declared in the Measurement configuration. Secondly, the Whitelist updater updates whitelist values to the Open CIT database and pass on t-PCR value to the PCR-signed kernel generator.

Using the TUX Whitelist updater, TUX maintains up-to-date whitelist with the values produced by the Whitelist updater. Because the whitelist values are self-produced and updated within the attestation server, TUX prevents attestation failure after system updates. Figure 2A illustrates a comparison between regular open CIT remote attestation and TUX remote attestation.

PCR-signed kernel generator generates PCR-signed kernel by leveraging Secure boot sign tool [7]. PCR-signed kernel generator takes t-PCR from the Whitelist updater and encrypts it with the TUX owner's private key. The encrypted value gets stored into the digital signature and appended to the kernel binary from the Trusted repository. Then, the finalized the PCR-signed kernel is deployed to the local machine. The following section will further explain the PCR-signed kernel in detail.

PCR-signed Kernel. The PCR-signed kernel is a unique kernel that contains integrity information of the managed system. As shown in the Fig. 3, a PCR-signed kernel is comprised of a kernel binary and a digital signature, which holds encrypted t-PCR. Using the PCR-signed kernel, TUX can easily deploy known-good integrity value to the managed machines. TUX mandates each managed machine to use the PCR-signed kernel. The PCR-signed kernel is used in PCR-verification to verify the integrity of the system's booting process, instead of LCP. Details about the PCR-verification is mentioned at the following section.

TUX-Secure Boot (TS-boot). TS-boot is a batch of booting schemes collaborate to enable verified and measured booting scheme. It is composed of UEFI

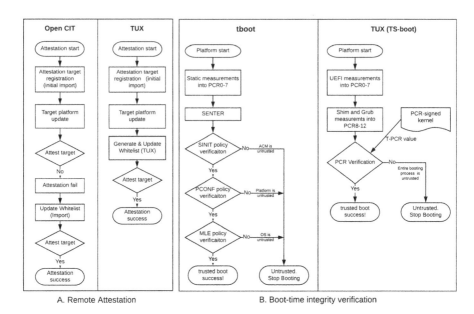

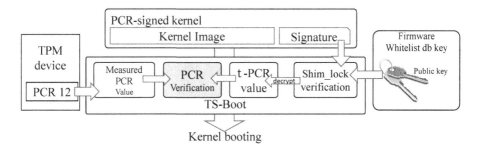

Fig. 2. Comparison between TUX, Open CIT, and tboot

Fig. 3. The PCR-verification components and its process

secure boot, Shim, and Trusted Grub. Note that the Grub is the most popular Linux bootloader, and thus, TUX maximizes Linux compatibility. By utilizing TS-boot, TUX can guarantee the robust and strict integrity of Linux booting process. TS-boot takes place in the managed machine as shown in Fig. 1.

TS-boot provides three services to guarantee the integrity of managed machine's booting process. First of all, TS-boot uses firmware keys to verify booting components. TS-boot adopts *Shim*, the first-stage bootloader, to perform firmware level integrity check. Shim bootloader defines a function to use firmware key verification, called shim_lock verification. Using the shim_lock verification, TS-boot verifies every component used in the Linux booting (e.g., Grub, OS kernel, and Initrd) with keys stored in the firmware.

Second, TS-boot enforces integrity measurement using TPM from the beginning of booting to OS kernel. As soon as the booting starts, the UEFI secure boot measures hardware and BIOS configurations to first eight PCR registers respectively. Then, the UEFI BIOS verifies and executes Shim, Shim measures and verifies Grub, OS kernel, and initrd binary before execution. Finally, the Trusted Grub measures Grub configuration file and executed Grub commands. Note that all values are extended from the measurements from the previous stage.

Lastly, TS-boot introduces *PCR-verification* to guarantee the strict and robust integrity of the entire booting process. PCR-verification verifies the integrity of the booting process by comparing TPM measurements of the entire booting process against the *t-PCR* in the kernel's signature. Figure 3 shows the overall PCR-verification process. TS-Boot measures all the hardware configuration, executed binaries, and Grub commands are extended to the PCR12 so that it can capture the integrity of the entire booting process. Therefore, if anything of the above components or sequences change, the value of the PCR12 also changes. To achieve *t-PCR* value, TS-boot decrypts the encrypted *t-PCR* value in the signature using the TUX owner's public key stored in the firmware db. Then, by comparing the value of the PCR12 against the *t-PCR* TS-boot verifies the thorough integrity of the booting process. TS-Boot allows kernel execution only when the two values are matched, meaning that the hardware configurations and software executions are intact and not compromised. Figure 2B presents a comparison of boot-time verification with tboot and TUX.

5 Implementation

5.1 Integrity Manager

PCR Calculation. TPM 2.0 provides multiple hash algorithms for measuring the integrity of the platform. For TUX, the SHA-256 algorithm was used for calculating the *t-PCR* value and the up-to-date whitelist. This is because, recently, SHA-1 collision [12] was announced, and most security vendors suggest not to use SHA-1 but use SHA-2 algorithms for robust security.

For PCR calculation, TUX owner first configures the Measurement configuration. Then, the whitelist values and *t-PCR* is calculated according to the Measurement configuration by using the PCR extend operation. The PCR extend operation is defined as follows:

$$PCR_{new} = H(PCR_{previous} \oplus H(Data))$$

where H() is a TPM's hash function, which calculates SHA-256 hash, and $\oplus$ is a concatenation operator. The PCR extend operation takes the value from the previous stage and data of the current stage to extend integrity values. By following the operations defined in the Measurement configuration.

PCR-signing. PCR-signed kernel generator utilizes Secure Boot signing tool, SB-signing tool [7], to make a digital signature. The generator takes three inputs: OS kernel binary, *t-PCR* value, and TUX owner's private key. To generate the signed kernel, PCR-signed kernel generator first encrypts the *t-PCR*, instead of the digested hash of a file, with the TUX owner's private key. Then the encrypted value is combined in to a digital signature and appended to the kernel binary creating the PCR-signed kernel. The produced PCR-signed kernel is deployed to the managed machine and update the system. Note that the TUX PCR-signed kernel generator runs inside the attestation server, which should be safe and trustworthy. Therefore, vital assets such as TUX owner's private key are secure.

5.2   TS-Boot

PCR Read. Reading the PCR on the run is essential for PCR-verification. However, reading the PCR value of TPM 2.0 was not implemented in the Shim, where PCR-verification is conducted. Thus, PCR read operation was added to the Shim. Note that TPM 2.0's PCR implementation is more sophisticated than TPM 1.2.

PCR Usages. There are multiple PCRs inside TPM. In our implementation, we measure the platform integrity to PCRs from PCR0–PCR12. Table 1 explains each PCR usages.

TPM Measurements. For integrity verification, additional TPM measurements are added to Shim and Trusted Grub. First of all, we added measurements for the Grub, kernel, and initrd in the Shim to accurately measure each binary to the PCRs described in Table 1. Also, more measurements are added to extend entire booting process to the PCR12. To begin with, Shim merges the hardware PCR values to the PCR12. PCR0–PCR7 are consecutively read and extended to PCR12. Then, along with the booting process, all the TPM measurements are additionally extended to PCR12, generating the integrity hash of the entire booting process. All the measurements are measured with the SHA-256 algorithm for the brevity.

Table 1. Platform configuration register (PCR) usages

PCR	Contents	Measurment host
PCR0-7	BIOS and hardware configurations	UEFI Secure boot
PCR8	Executed Grub commands	Trusted Grub
PCR9	Executed modules from Trusted Grub	Trusted Grub
PCR10	Trusted Grub binary	Shim
PCR11	Kernel and initrd	Shim
PCR12	Entire booting process	UEFI Secure boot, Trusted Grub, and Shim

PCR-verification. To implement PCR-verification, we adopt shim_lock verification, which is part of the shim_lock protocol. The shim_lock protocol allows Grub to communicate with the Shim, which has access to firmware database.

The PCR-verification is located at the *linuxefi* command, which is a Grub command to load kernel and initrd, to verify the kernel and the boot process before kernel execution. After the kernel is loaded to the memory, it is sent to Shim using the shim_lock protocol. Then Shim measures the binary to the PCR12. After the measurement, as shown in the following pseudo code, the value of PCR12 is read and compared against the decrypted signature, the *t-PCR*. If the verification fails, the kernel execution halts and TUX discards booting.

```
pcrval;
TPM_readPCR(12,pcrval); //read pcr12
...
// decrypt signature using the firmware db key.
// compare read pcr12 and the decrypted value.
if (check_db_cert(cert, pcrval)) {
    console_notify(L"PCR Verification Success :)\n");
    return EFI_SUCCESS;
} else {
    console_notify(L"PCR Verification Fail\n");
    return EFI_FAIL;
}
```

PCR-verification provides robust integrity, forbidding all changes during the booting. Also, it uses one value, *t-PCR*, to verify whole booting process, taking advantage of the chain-of-trust.

5.3   Kernel Update Procedure

TUX defines specific kernel update procedure for the managed machines to properly manage integrity according to the updates. The overall update process of TUX is shown in Fig. 4.

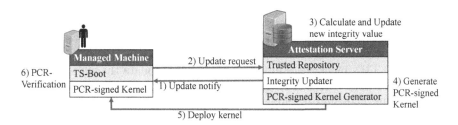

Fig. 4. The TUX update procedure

First of all, kernel update repository, defined in each managed machine's sign.list, is set to TUX's Trusted repository. Thus, when a new kernel is released, the user is notified of the new kernel from the Trusted repository.

Second, the update process is triggered by the user. When the update is requested, the attestation server checks the registered information of the managed machine. Hence, the server is aware of managed machine's update state transparently.

Third, the attestation server's Integrity manager calculates Trusted PCR value (t-PCR) the Measurement configuration and the requested binary. Note that the new whitelist value is derived and updated at this stage, and thus, the attestation server has up-to-date known-good value.

Fourth, the t-PCR is passed on to PCR-signed kernel generator. With the t-PCR and the valid kernel binary from the Trusted repository, the PCR-signed kernel is generated.

Finally, the PCR-signed kernel is distributed over the network. The local admin receives and installs the new kernel, finishing the update procedure of TUX. Also, the Grub configuration is updated to adopt new kernel.

5.4   Installation of TS-Boot

The initial installation of TS-Boot is vital because it set the initial root-of-trust. At the initial installation, the IT department (TUX owner) gathers essential information about the managed machine. The initial installation only needs to be performed once.

Initial installation of the TS-boot is conducted in following steps:

First, the managed machine admin checks hardware requirements of its platform. A managed machine should have TPM 2.0, and UEFI BIOS with secure boot.

Second, the managed machine admin enrolls the TUX owner's public key to the firmware db of the platform and enables the secure boot. This step is essential to provide root-of-trust and firmware level integrity verification.

Third, to achieve UUID of the boot partition, the managed machine admin installs normal Linux distribution without TS-Boot.

Fourth, the managed machine admin performs initial registration to the attestation server. Here the attestation server imports PCR values and UUID.

Fifth, the TUX owner generates the whitelist values, the PCR-signed kernel, and corresponding Grub configuration file using the TUX integrity manager. The Grub configuration file is driven from the TUX owner's Measurement configuration.

Sixth, the TUX owner uses integrity manager to update the whitelist values and deploy TS-boot with PCR-signed kernel and Grub configuration.

Finally, the managed machine admin installs TS-boot by updating Shim, Grub, Grub configuration file, and kernel image.

6   Experiments

6.1   TPM Measurements

TUX TS-boot measures PCR values along with the booting process. The measurement values of the managed machine are stored in the PCRs. The measured values are then compared with the whitelist values in the attestation server. If the measurements do not match, the attestation server states the machine is not trustworthy.

In this experiment, we show changes in PCR values according to hardware, bios configuration, and executed kernel. Figure 5 shows the result of four different settings. The settings are configured as follow: (**A**) Hardware 1 + Secure boot on + kernel version vmlinuz-4.4.0-104, (**B**) Hardware 1 + Secure boot on + kernel version vmlinuz-4.4.0-109, (**C**) Hardware 1 + Secure boot off + kernel version vmlinuz-4.4.0-109, (**D**) Hardware 2 + Secure boot on + kernel version vmlinuz-4.4.0-109.

The comparison between configuration **A** and **B** shows PCR change due to the kernel update. Using the PC 1, we updated the kernel from vmlinuz-4.4.0-104 to vmlinuz-4.4.0-109. This caused changes in PCR8, 11, and 12 since the binary content and the kernel loading commands line[1] is modified. Also, PCR11 for configuration **B** and **D** remains the same because they use same Kernel and initrd binary, version 4.4.0-109.

The comparison between configuration **B** and **C** shows PCR changes due to BIOS modification, turning Secure boot on and off. This experiment causes changes in PCR7 and 12. Also, turning Secure boot off disables shim_lock verification. Thus PCR11 was not measured.

The comparison between **C** and **D** illustrates different hardware (PC) having different PCR values for PCR1 and PCR5. Finally, the PCR1, 5, and 11 are different between **A** and **D** since the kernel is changed as well as the hardware.

Additionally, we can see that all configurations have the same values for PCR 10 and 9 because we have used same Grub binary and modules. Furthermore, PCR12, which is used for PCR-verification, is unique for all configurations.

A. PC1+SB on+Kernel 104	B. PC1+SB on+Kernel 109	C. PC1+SB off+Kernel 109	D. PC2+SB on+Kernel 109
Bank/Algorithm: TPM ALG SHA256(0x000b)			
PCR_00: 05 48 02 7e c	PCR_00: 05 48 02 7e c	PCR_00: 05 48 02 7e cf	PCR_00: 05 48 02 7e cf
PCR_01: f1 67 99 3b a	PCR_01: f1 67 99 3b a	PCR_01: f1 67 99 3b a5	PCR_01: c7 84 e6 09 94
PCR_02: 3d 45 8c fe 5	PCR_02: 3d 45 8c fe 5	PCR_02: 3d 45 8c fe 55	PCR_02: 3d 45 8c fe 55
PCR_03: 3d 45 8c fe 5	PCR_03: 3d 45 8c fe 5	PCR_03: 3d 45 8c fe 55	PCR_03: 3d 45 8c fe 55
PCR_04: f5 f8 1f 6b 5	PCR_04: f5 f8 1f 6b 5	PCR_04: f5 f8 1f 6b 5b	PCR_04: f5 f8 1f 6b 5b
PCR_05: de 89 35 69 c	PCR_05: de 89 35 69 c	PCR_05: de 89 35 69 c2	PCR_05: 39 55 01 58 89
PCR_06: 3d 45 8c fe 5	PCR_06: 3d 45 8c fe 5	PCR_06: 3d 45 8c fe 55	PCR_06: 3d 45 8c fe 55
PCR_07: 25 c0 b3 ce 4	PCR_07: 25 c0 b3 ce 4	PCR_07: 47 d9 c1 f4 d9	PCR_07: 25 c0 b3 ce 45
PCR_08: 63 81 11 5c d	PCR_08: f4 1e 86 df 9	PCR_08: b1 5d 09 67 39	PCR_08: a6 fe 12 0a 0f
PCR_09: e2 fa 1b a3 f	PCR_09: e2 fa 1b a3 f	PCR_09: e2 fa 1b a3 f9	PCR_09: e2 fa 1b a3 f9
PCR_10: 0b 74 50 53 8	PCR_10: 0b 74 50 53 8	PCR_10: 0b 74 50 53 8e	PCR_10: 0b 74 50 53 8e
PCR_11: 53 45 a7 13 8	PCR_11: 79 bd 24 78 8	PCR_11: 00 00 00 00 00	PCR_11: 79 bd 24 78 88
PCR_12: 92 5a 80 6e c	PCR_12: 31 68 59 c3 e	PCR_12: 10 5e fc 8c b1	PCR_12: 76 fc 4d 87 a9

Fig. 5. PCR measurements for different configurations.

---

[1] The Grub's kernel loading command includes the version of the kernel.

6.2   PCR-verification

In this experiment, we show robust security enforcement using the PCR-verification. Adjustment in hardware, BIOS configuration, booting commands, and binaries cause modification of PCR12. When booting components are modified, the PCR12 value changes, as shown in Fig. 5.

Figure 6a shows modification in Grub configuration file (Grub.cfg), which also caused Measured value to change. Thus, when *t-PCR* and modified PCR12 value is compared, TS-boot halts booting, concluding that the integrity of the booting is broken. Figure 6b shows verification fail message produced by the Shim.

6.3   Whitelist Update

In this experiment, we show whitelist update, integrity value generation, and attestation result using up-to-date whitelist value. Note that, we experimented only with the PCR12 (*t-PCR*) to simplify the experiment. To update the whitelist, we defined a Measurement configuration according to Ubuntu 16.04's

(a) Modified Grub.cfg   (b) Fail message from Shim

Fig. 6. PCR-verification

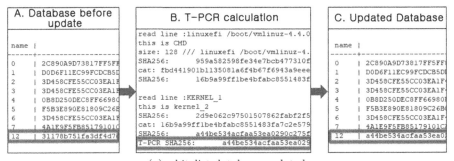

(a) whitelist database updated.

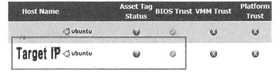

(b) Attestation Success for BIOS.

Fig. 7. Attestation with updated whitelist

booting process. Using the Measurement configuration, we generated *t-PCR*. Then, we updated whitelist in the Open CIT database with SQL update statement.

Figure 7a-A shows whitelist database before the update, Fig. 7a-B illustrates *t-PCR* calculation using different kernel version, and Fig. 7a-C is the whitelist database which is updated with the *t-PCR*. Finally, Fig. 7b illustrates attestation success for the BIOS, which refers to the booting process, after the update.

7 Discussion

7.1 Recovery from Broken Integrity

Integrity can be broken when the user unintentionally modifies the booting component. In this case, the system should re-install the TS-boot and the kernel. Even when the integrity is broken, TUX provides simple recovery procedure compared to Intel TXT. Table 2 compares recovery procedure of TUX and tboot.

Table 2. Recovery procedure comparison of TUX and tboot.

	TUX	tboot
1	Restore original TS-boot binaries (Grub, kernel, etc.)	TPM clear to take ownership
2	Restore Grub configuration	Re-install SINIT
3	–	Restore original binaries (Grub, kernel, etc.)
4	–	Restore Grub configuration
5	–	Reset Launch Control Policy
6	–	Update TPM NVRAM

7.2 Roll-Back and Multiple Kernel Support

TUX can support version roll-back and multiple kernels. As long as the requested version is stored in the Trusted repository, a user can request specific kernel version to roll-back. Moreover, TUX supports using multiple versions of kernels at the same time by defining multiple kernel information in the Grub configuration file. At boot-time, a user can select kernel version to boot from the Grub menu.

Also, TUX can support attestation for multiple kernels. When the client is attested, it can provide kernel version information in the quote to the attestation server. Then the server updates the whitelist according to the provided kernel version with the Integrity manager. After the whitelist update, the attestation server can successfully attest the client's integrity.

Additionally, TUX is robust to roll-back attacks, in which the adversary replacing a trusted version with an old vulnerable version. TUX trusted repository holds trusted versions of Linux kernel and TUX is capable of version-based remote attestation as mentioned above. Thus, the roll-back attack can be detected by remote attestation.

7.3   TUX Owner's Public Key

TUX requires every managed system to have TUX owner's public key installed to the firmware db. The installed key is used as a root-of-trust. We assume that the firmware is protected and difficult to be modified, and thus, the key is safe. Even though the public key is modified and the booting is compromised, with remote attestation, we can detect changes in the TPM measurement and state the system untrusted.

8   Conclusion

This paper presents the design and implementation of TUX, the Trust Update on Linux booting. With TUX, we handle integrity seriously as much as updates to secure the system. TUX integrates update server to the Open CIT to transparently manage system updates. Also, TUX performs remote attestation with the up-to-date whitelist, eliminating misguided attestation failure caused by updates.

Furthermore, TUX provides robust verified and measured boot with TS-Boot. TS-Boot verifies thorough integrity regarding the Linux booting process using the PCR-verification. With TS-Boot, a system can validate hardware environment, BIOS, bootloaders, executed Grub commands, and OS kernel binary. Thus, by utilizing TUX, we can successfully manage the integrity of the platform along with updates.

References

1. Neus, D.: Rohde-schwarz-cybersecurity/trustedGRUB2: TPM enabled GRUB2 bootloader, June 2017. https://github.com/Rohde-Schwarz-Cybersecurity/TrustedGrub2
2. Futral, W., Greene, J.: Intel Trusted Execution Technology for Server Platforms: A Guide to More Secure Data Centers, 1st edn. Apress, Berkely (2013)
3. Sharkey, J.: Breaking hardware-enforced security with hypervisors. In: Black Hat USA (2016). https://www.blackhat.com/docs/us-16/materials/us-16-Sharkey-Breaking-Hardware-Enforced-Security-With-Hypervisors.pdf
4. Kleissner, P.: Stoned bootkit. Black Hat USA (2009). http://www.blackhat.com/presentations/bh-usa-09/KLEISSNER/BHUSA09-Kleissner-StonedBootkit-SLIDES.pdf
5. Kocher, P., et al.: Spectre attacks: exploiting speculative execution. ArXiv e-prints, January 2018
6. Lipp, M., et al.: Meltdown. ArXiv e-prints, January 2018
7. Sekletar, M.: Sbsigntool github. https://github.com/msekletar/sbsigntool
8. Microsoft: Protect your windows devices against spectre meltdown, April 2018. https://support.microsoft.com/ko-kr/help/4073757/protect-your-windows-devices/against-spectre-meltdown
9. Red Hat Bootloader Team: UEFI Shim loader. https://github.com/rhboot/Shim
10. Redhat: RHSA-2018:0093 - security advisory, January 2018. https://access.redhat.com/errata/RHSA-2018:0093

11. Savino, R.: Open cit 3.2.1 product guide. opencit/opencit wiki, February 2018. https://github.com/opencit/opencit/wiki/Open-CIT-3.2.1-Product-Guide
12. Stevens, M., Bursztein, E., Karpman, P., Albertini, A., Markov, Y.: The first collision for full SHA-1. In: Katz, J., Shacham, H. (eds.) CRYPTO 2017. LNCS, vol. 10401, pp. 570–596. Springer, Cham (2017). https://doi.org/10.1007/978-3-319-63688-7_19
13. Trusted Computing Group: TCG architecture overview, version 1.4, August 2007. https://trustedcomputinggroup.org/tcg-architecture-overview/version-1-4/. Accessed 02 July 2018
14. Trusted Computing Group: TPM main specification, October 2014. https://trustedcomputinggroup.org/tpm-main-specification/
15. UEFI: Unified extensible firmware interface specification, January 2016. http://www.uefi.org/sites/default/files/resources/UEFI%20Spec%202_6.pdf
16. Wei, J., Wang, S., Sun, N., Qiaowei, R.: Trusted boot—sourceforge.net. https://sourceforge.net/projects/tboot/

Verifiable Outsourcing of Computations Using Garbled Onions

Tahsin C. M. Dönmez$^{(\boxtimes)}$ (iD)

Department of Future Technologies, University of Turku, Turku, Finland
`tcmdon@utu.fi`

Abstract. Solutions to the verifiable outsourcing problem based on Yao's Garbled Circuit (GC) construction have been investigated in previous works. A major obstacle to the practicality of these solutions is the single-use nature of the GC construction. This work introduces the novel technique *onion garbling*, which circumvents this obstacle by using only a symmetric-key cipher as its cryptographic machinery. This work also proposes a non-interactive protocol for verifiable outsourcing which utilizes the onion garbling technique. The protocol works in a 3-party setting, and consists of a preprocessing phase and an online phase. The cost of a preprocessing phase which can support up to N computations is independent of N for the outsourcing party. For the other two parties, the memory and communication cost of N-reusability is proportional to $N \cdot m$, where m is the bit-length of the input. The cost of input preparation and verification is $\mathcal{O}(m + n)$ symmetric-key cipher operations, where n is the bit-length of the output. The overall costs associated with the outsourcing party are low enough to allow verifiable outsourcing of arbitrary computations by resource-constrained devices on constrained networks. Finally, this work reports on a proof-of-concept implementation of the proposed verifiable outsourcing protocol.

Keywords: Verifiable computation · Outsourcing · Garbled onion

1 Introduction

Verifiable outsourcing of computations involves a possibly computationally weak outsourcing party (outsourcer), and one or more worker parties (evaluators) who are possibly untrusted by the outsourcer. The outsourcer sends the inputs for the computation to the evaluator, and the evaluator sends back the result of the computation along with some additional information which enables the outsourcer to verify the received result. How much the outsourcer benefits from outsourcing depends on how much less the cost of verification is compared to the cost of performing the computation, $Cost_C$. Obviously, if the cost of verification is greater than or equal to $Cost_C$, the outsourcer would rather perform the

This work is supported in part by Tekes.

S. K. Katsikas and C. Alcaraz (Eds.): STM 2018, LNCS 11091, pp. 122–137, 2018.
https://doi.org/10.1007/978-3-030-01141-3_8

computation itself. It is also desirable that, the cost of the verifiable computation to the evaluator is as close as possible to $Cost_C$.

Current and emerging trends such as cloud computing, fog computing, and more recently, multi-access edge computing (MEC) increase the interest in finding solutions to the verifiable computation problem. Furthermore, the number of computationally weak devices have increased drastically in recent years due to the ongoing realization of the Internet of Things (IoT).

There are different approaches to the verifiable computation problem. Some solutions target specific computations, whereas others are general-purpose solutions which allow arbitrary computations. Efficiency of general purpose solutions based on probabilistically checkable proofs and fully-homomorphic encryption are not yet at the acceptable level for practical applications, and the efforts to reduce the verification cost below the cost of computation continue [16]. There are also general-purpose solutions which are based on Yao's Garbled Circuit (GC) construction [18,19]. These solutions enjoy the non-interactivity and inherent verifiability of secure 2-party computations using GCs. In this case, the verification can be as simple as comparing a key value $k_{revealed}$ with two others k^0 and k^1, where the verification succeeds if and only if $k_{revealed} \in \{k^0, k^1\}$.[1] However, the single-use nature of the GC construction is a major obstacle to practical verifiable outsourcing using GCs. Following an evaluation, the evaluator learns either $k_{revealed} = k^0$ or $k_{revealed} = k^1$. If the same GC is reused for a second evaluation, nothing stops the evaluator from submitting the output key revealed in the first evaluation ($k_{revealed}$), even though the second evaluation revealed $k'_{revealed} \neq k_{revealed}$. Because the GC is reused, $k'_{revealed} \in \{k^0, k^1\}$, and the verifiability property is lost.

In many cases, using a new garbled circuit for each computation is not practical, as Boolean circuits for non-trivial computations can be quite large, resulting in unacceptable memory and communication costs. Achieving full reusability in GC-based protocols is possible [7,8], however these solutions rely on (relatively) costly cryptographic techniques such as fully-homomorphic encryption and functional encryption. In case of full reusability, the cost associated with the construction of the single GC can be amortized over several computations. This work introduces the *onion garbling* technique, which provides N-reusability using only a symmetric-key cipher. In case of N-reusability, N computations still require N GC constructions, however the memory and communication costs are limited to those of a single GC, plus a term which is independent of the circuit size. This work also proposes a protocol for verifiable outsourcing of computations, which utilizes the onion garbling technique. The protocol: (1) is non-interactive in the sense that the outsourcer's online time complexity is linear in the input length; (2) does not provide privacy of inputs, outputs, or the computation; (3) works in a 3-party setting, and consists of a preprocessing phase and an online phase. The construction of a garbled onion (of N layers) is carried out in the preprocessing phase by a computationally capable party (constructor) that is trusted by the outsourcer. The cost of a preprocessing phase which can sup-

---

[1] For simplicity, a single output wire is assumed.

port up to N computations is $\mathcal{O}(K)$ for the outsourcing party, where K is the security parameter (key size of the GC). The memory and communication cost for the other two parties is $\mathcal{O}(|C| \cdot R + N \cdot m \cdot K)$, where $|C|$ is the number of gates in the Boolean circuit, R is the ciphertext size for the encryption scheme used for encrypting the circuit, and m is the bit-length of the input. For large circuits, this is significantly smaller compared to the cost of constructing and transferring N independent garbled circuits, which is $\mathcal{O}(|C| \cdot R \cdot N)$. In other words, N-reusability is achieved at a cost proportional to $N \cdot m$. The cost of input preparation and verification to the outsourcer is $\mathcal{O}(m + n)$ symmetric-key cipher operations, where n is the bit-length of the output. The overall costs associated with the outsourcer are low enough to allow verifiable outsourcing of arbitrary computations by resource-constrained devices on constrained networks [11].

The rest of this paper is organized as follows. Section 2 mentions related works. Section 3 describes the onion garbling technique. Section 4 presents the proposed protocol, and Sect. 5 discusses its security. Section 6 reports on the implementation of the protocol. Sections 7 and 8 conclude the paper and discuss future work.

2   Related Work

Applebaum et al. [1] show how to convert the privacy property in secure multi-party computation to verifiability, using MACs and symmetric encryption. Ishai et al. [10] define partial garbling schemes, where the security goals of garbling schemes [3] are relaxed. They propose a verifiable computation scheme building upon the garble + MAC paradigm of [1], where the only private input is a one-time MAC, and the rest of the inputs are public.

Gennaro et al. [7] note that Yao's GC Construction provides a one-time verifiable computation, in addition to providing secure two-party computation. In the same work [7], they formalize the notion of verifiable computation, and propose a protocol for verifiable outsourcing of computations, which uses fully-homomorphic encryption to overcome the single-use nature of the GCs.

3   How to Garble Onions

A garbled onion is a construction built upon a stripped down version of Yao's garbled circuits. A single garbled onion, or simply onion, consists of N layers of garbled circuits. The construction features two operations *AddLayer* and *Peel*. *AddLayer* operation adds a new GC to the onion, placing it at the outermost layer. As a result, the GC which was previously at the outermost layer is wrapped and no longer exposed. Each GC added via an *AddLayer* operation is constructed in a way that depends on the GC at the layer immediately below. This dependency allows the peeling of onion layers via the *Peel* operation, which removes the outermost layer to expose the layer below.

While the description above is useful for introducing the idea, the construction would not be as useful if it were merely a collection of co-existing GCs, as suggested by the mental image of an onion. Thanks to the dependency between the consecutive layers, an onion is fully defined by the single GC at its outermost layer, the input mappings for each layer, and two seed values. What *AddLayer* actually does is the transformation of this single GC, so working on a single circuit object suffices for the construction of an onion. Similarly, the *Peel* operation is the transformation of the single GC at the outermost layer into the GC at the lower layer. Consequently, the communication of only one GC (plus the input mappings for each layer, and the two seed values) is sufficient for N verifiable computations, where N is the number of onion layers. Figure 1 depicts a 3-layer garbled onion.

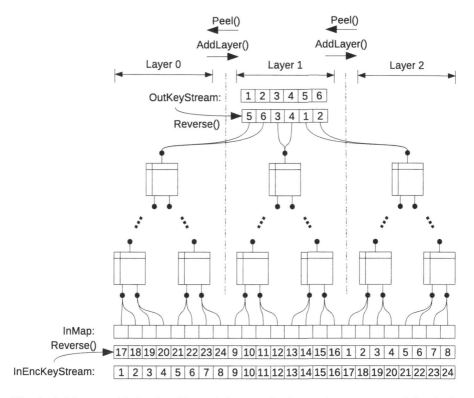

Fig. 1. A 3-layer garbled onion. For each layer, only the two input gates and the single output gate are shown. Numbers inside the boxes indicate the order of generation within the stream.

Before we move on to describe the construction, evaluation, and peeling of garbled onions in the following subsections, we explain what we mean by a stripped down version of Yao's GC.[2] In Yao's garbled circuit construction, each wire is assigned two keys k^0 and k^1 corresponding to the two possible wire

---

[2] A more formal definition will also be given in Sect. 5 (See Definition 1).

values 0 and 1, respectively. For each gate g_r, the keys k_s^0, k_s^1, k_t^0, and k_t^1 are used to double-encrypt the keys k_r^0 and k_r^1, where each one of s and t is either a gate index for a gate whose output wire is connected to an input wire of g_r (we will refer to such a gate as a *child gate* in the rest of the paper), or an index of an input wire for the circuit. The two encryption keys and the key to be encrypted are chosen respecting the structure of the truth table (TT), so that the evaluation of the garbled circuit with the garbled inputs mimics the in-the-clear evaluation with the corresponding non-garbled inputs. This process yields the encrypted truth table (ETT) for the gate (see Fig. 2). There are two components that exist in Yao's GC construction, but not in the garbled onion construction: row shuffling and row selection.[3] Yao's GC construction involves the additional step of shuffling the rows of the ETTs, so that the values on a gate's input wires cannot be inferred from the index of the row opened during the evaluation. Furthermore, evaluation of a GC requires at each gate the selection of the row which should be decrypted using the keys assigned to the gate's input wires. Row selection is achieved via trial and error (only possible if authenticated encryption is used), or via the point-and-permute technique [2]. In order to have the verifiability property, it is sufficient that an evaluation with a particular set of garbled inputs exposes one and only one of the keys for each non-input wire of the circuit. When one is concerned solely with verifiability, all requirements about privacy can be dropped, and hiding neither the orderings of ETT rows, nor the truth tables is necessary. Therefore, the GCs in a garbled onion do not have their ETT rows shuffled, and during the evaluation of an onion layer we let the in-the-clear evaluation of the circuit guide the row selections.

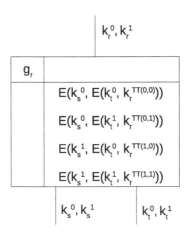

Fig. 2. An encrypted gate. Note that the rows are not shuffled.

---

[3] Even though the construction involves the encryption of TTs rather than full garbling thereof, it is named as *Garbled Onion* in order to make its close connection with garbled circuits apparent.

3.1 Construction

Construction of an N-layered onion involves successively (N times) adding layers via the *AddLayer* operation. The resulting garbled onion consists of the garbled circuit C_o (which is the GC at the outermost layer), the input mappings *InMap*, the seed value *SeedInEncKeyStream* (which generates the keystream *InEncKeyStream*), and the seed value *SeedOutKeyStream* (which generates the keystream *OutKeyStream*). *InMap* holds the key values (both k^0 and k^1) that are assigned to the input wires of the GC at each layer, whereas *OutKeyStream* determines for every layer the key values that are assigned to the output wires of the GC. *SeedInEncKeyStream* and the corresponding stream *InEncKeyStream* are optional components of the construction. *InEncKeyStream* is a stream of encryption keys which are used for encrypting the input mappings *InMap*. Encryption of the input mappings is necessary, for example, when their transfer between two mutually trusting parties have to involve an untrusted third party as a conveyor.

All keys of a GC can be assigned values freely. Traditionally, this fact is taken advantage of in GC optimizations such as the free-XOR technique [13] and garbled row reduction [15], which make the keys in the same circuit inter-dependent, or fix some of the keys to some known value. For a GC in an onion, the keys associated with the output wires are assigned from *OutKeyStream*, however every other key can be assigned values freely. We will refer to these keys as *assignable keys*. Garbled onion construction takes advantage of this freedom by making the garbled circuits in neighbouring layers inter-dependent. During the formation of layer l via the $(l + 1)^{\text{th}}$ *AddLayer* operation, ETT rows of C_o are stored in the assignable keys,[4] and the keys associated with the output wires are assigned values from *OutKeyStream*. The assignable keys associated with the input wires of the circuit are stored in *InMap*. Finally, ETT rows are overridden by encrypting the circuit with the new keys, and the new transformed C_o is obtained.

Clearly, onion garbling requires that there are enough bits in the assignable keys to store all ETT rows. The number of ETT rows for a garbled gate is equal to the number of keys associated with the input wires for single-input gates (such as *NOT* and *NAND*) and two-input gates (such as *AND* and *XOR*), and greater in any other case. Assuming that the size of ETT rows is equal to the key size K, if one or more gates in a circuit has more than two inputs, there won't be enough bits to store all ETT rows. There exists functionally complete sets whose elements accept either one or two inputs (e.g. $\{AND, XOR\}$, $\{AND, NOT\}$, $\{NAND\}$). Therefore no constraints are posed with regard to which functions are suitable for onion garbling and which are not.

The rules that guide the actual assignments of assignable keys can be chosen arbitrarily. In our implementation (see Sect. 6), ETT row size is equal to K (due to the use of one-time-pad for encrypting TT rows) and the total number of ETT rows is equal to total number of assignable keys (because we restrict ourselves

---

[4] During the formation of the innermost layer (i.e. for $l = 0$), there are no ETT rows to store, so the assignable keys are assigned random values.

to gates with 2 inputs). We chose to assign the ETT rows of a gate to the keys associated with the input wires of that gate. With regard to ordering, keys associated with the left wire are assigned from the upper rows of the ETT, and between two keys which are associated with the same wire, the key corresponding to value 0 is assigned from the upper row of the ETT. Figure 3 depicts the assignment of the assignable keys according to these rules during an *AddLayer* operation.

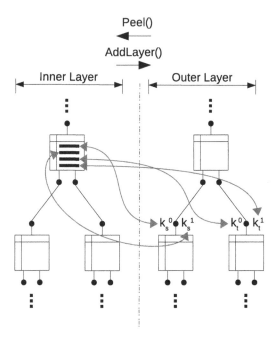

Fig. 3. The mapping between the ETT rows of a parent gate and the keys associated with the output wires of its children, during *AddLayer* and *Peel* operations.

The assignment from *OutKeyStream* to the keys associated with output wires follow a particular rule in order to allow the possibly resource-constrained outsourcer to generate, use, and discard keys one at a time as they become needed during the verifications of the computations for subsequent layers. The stream has to be accessed from opposite ends during the construction and during the computations, as the layers are traversed in reverse order: the innermost layer of the onion is the first layer that is constructed, and it is used in the very last outsourced computation. The computationally capable constructor takes the burden of reversing the order, so that the outsourcer can use the keys in the order they are generated from the stream. The same is also true for *InEncKeyStream*. During the encryption of the input mappings, *InEncKeyStream* is accessed in reverse order, so that the outsourcer can generate, use, and discard encryption keys one at a time as they become needed during the preparation of garbled inputs for subsequent layers. For both streams, the keys associated with the same layer are treated as a block, and the reversal of streams during construction occur only at the block level (See Fig. 1).

Note that the reversal of $InEncKeyStream$ and $OutKeyStream$ is not necessary if they can flow in both directions, i.e. if it is possible to efficiently obtain not only the next stream element, but also the previous one. Whether or not a stream can flow in both directions depends on the cryptographic machinery used. Using AES-CTR [5] with a combination of layer index and gate index as counter allows random access to the generated keystream, which is more than what is needed: a keystream which flows in both directions. In this case, the outsourcer is able to follow the streams backwards one AES operation at a time, so the constructor does not need to reverse them.

3.2   Evaluation

The evaluation of an onion layer, i.e. the evaluation of the garbled circuit C_o using the garbled inputs, is almost identical to regular garbled circuit evaluation except a few differences. The gates of C_o are visited in the usual order. Before a visited garbled gate is evaluated, the corresponding gate in the un-garbled circuit is evaluated, yielding an index i of the TT row, as well as the gate output read at that index. The selection of the ETT row to be decrypted is guided by the in-the-clear evaluation, i.e. the index of the ETT row that has to be decrypted is i. The key for decrypting this row is computed from the garbled outputs of its children, which are already visited and evaluated at this point. Decryption of the row yields the garbled output of the gate. Once all the gates are visited, garbled circuit evaluation is complete.

3.3   Peeling

Peeling removes the outermost layer to expose the GC at the layer below. Peeling can only be carried out when all the keys associated with the circuit's input wires are known. *Peel* operation involves going through the circuit gate by gate from inputs to outputs the same way as it is done during evaluation, but twice. During the first pass, at each gate g, the key that was not revealed during the evaluation is revealed. In order to do this, we first find an index i such that $TT(i) \neq v$, where v is the value output by g during the in-the-clear evaluation. Then, ETT row with index i is opened. This is possible because if g has a child gate, then it already went through this key-revealing process. The second pass through the circuit involves carrying out the assignments made during the *AddLayer* operation (corresponding to the layer being peeled) in reverse order (See Fig. 3). Using the assignable keys associated with the output wire of gate g, where one is revealed during evaluation, and the other one is revealed during the first pass through the circuit, half of the ETT rows for the parent gate of g is recovered. The other half is recovered using the keys associated with the output wire of the other child.

The reason why the circuit is traversed twice during peeling is that the re-evaluations using the ETTs and overwriting the ETTs of parent gates cannot be done in a single pass through the circuit (from children to parent), if we insist keeping memory usage to a single circuit size. Finally, note that at each layer of the onion, exactly two decryption operations are needed per gate: one during evaluation and the other during peeling.

4   Protocol for Verifiable Outsourcing Using Garbled Onions

In this section, we present a protocol for verifiable outsourcing of computations using garbled onions. The protocol works in a 3-party setting, and consists of a preprocessing phase (offline phase) and an online phase. The three parties involved are the outsourcer (a possibly computationally weak party who outsources the computations and verifies the results), the evaluator (a computationally capable untrusted party who performs the computation), and the constructor (a computationally capable trusted party who constructs the garbled onion).[5]

Before going into the details of the protocol, we briefly discuss why only the 3-party setting is considered. When the same party plays the role of both the constructor and the outsourcer, the protocol becomes applicable in the 2-party (outsourcer-evaluator) setting. In this case, it is not necessary to encrypt the input mappings or send them to the evaluator (See steps 5 and 6 of the preprocessing phase), but the outsourcer has to be capable of preparing, storing, and transferring the preprocessing material. Capable outsourcers exist, for example, in the realm of distributed computing projects such as SETI@home[6] and Folding@home[7], where computations are outsourced to CPUs and GPUs of volunteers over the Internet, and the possibility of dishonest evaluators makes verifiability desirable. The problem in this case is that the underlying onion garbling technique requires N circuit preparations for N computations, i.e. memory and communication costs are amortizable over several computations, but the computational cost is not. Therefore, the protocol does not provide practical benefits in the 2-party setting, unless the extra cost -due to the cost of preprocessing exceeding the cost of the computation- can be somehow justified.

The following subsections describe the preprocessing and online phases of the protocol.

4.1   Preprocessing Phase

This subsection describes a preprocessing phase which allows at most N verifiable outsourced computations. The constructor prepares all the preprocessing

---

[5] By (un)trusted we mean (un)trusted by the outsourcer.
[6] https://setiathome.berkeley.edu/.
[7] https://foldingathome.org/.

material without the involvement of the *outsourcer* and the *evaluator*, who may receive their share of the preprocessing material anytime before the first outsourced computation begins, and possibly at different times.

Preprocessing Phase

1. *Constructor* generates the non-garbled circuit C corresponding to the computation which will be outsourced.
2. *Constructor* generates two random seed values $SeedInEncKeyStream$ and $SeedOutKeyStream$, and uses them to initialize the streams $InEncKeyStream$ and $OutKeyStream$, respectively.
3. Let the number of input and output wires of C be m and n, respectively. *Constructor* generates the first $2 \cdot N \cdot m$ keys from $InEncKeyStream$, and the first $2 \cdot N \cdot n$ keys from $OutKeyStream$.
4. **Onion construction:** *Constructor* generates an N-layer garbled onion by N successive *AddLayer* operations (Section 3.1).
5. *Constructor* encrypts each key in the input mappings $InMap$ individually using the keys generated from $InEncKeyStream$, and obtains the encrypted input mappings $EncInMap$.
6. *Constructor* sends N, $EncInMap$, and C_o (the garbled circuit at the outermost layer) to the *evaluator*.
7. *Constructor* sends N, $SeedOutKeyStream$, and $SeedInEncKeyStream$ to the *outsourcer*.
8. *Evaluator* generates the non-garbled circuit C independently from the constructor (knowledge of the outsourced computation is sufficient for carrying out this task). Alternatively, C could be sent to the *evaluator* by the *constructor*.

4.2   Online Phase

This subsection describes the online phase for a single computation. Each one of the N possible computations follows the same steps. Parties involved in the online phase are the *outsourcer* and the *evaluator*. Both parties independently keep and maintain as internal state an index l, which is the index of the layer that will be used for the next computation. Initially, $l = N - 1$. The *outsourcer* initializes two keystreams $InEncKeyStream$ and $OutKeyStream$ with the seeds $SeedInEncKeyStream$ and $SeedOutKeyStream$, respectively. Internal state of the *outsourcer* includes, in addition to l, two key values: the last used values from each stream. Whenever the *outsourcer* needs an encryption key to decrypt an input mapping, or a key for verifying a received computation result, it simply gets the next key from the corresponding stream, and updates its internal state.

Online Phase

1. When the *outsourcer* wants to outsource a computation, it checks whether $l \geq 0$. If $l < 0$, verifiable outsourcing is not possible, and the protocol terminates. If $l \geq 0$, *outsourcer* initiates the computation by sending l to *evaluator*.

2. *Evaluator* checks whether both parties agree on the onion layer that will be used for the computation. In case of agreement, *evaluator* sends to *outsourcer* the encrypted input mappings for (only) layer l.
3. *Outsourcer* decrypts the input mappings using encryption keys generated from $InEncKeyStream$, revealing the garbled inputs g_i corresponding to its input bits b_i, as well as those corresponding to $\neg b_i$. We will refer to the latter as *unused garbled inputs* and denote them with g_i'. *Outsourcer* sends b_i and g_i to *evaluator*.
4. **Onion evaluation:** *Evaluator* evaluates the onion layer with index l using b_i and g_i (Section 3.2), and sends the computation result r (the keys associated with the output wires of the circuit) to *outsourcer*.
5. *Outsourcer* interprets and verifies the received computation result r. Let r_j be the key associated with the jth output wire. For each j:
   - *Outsourcer* generates two keys from $OutKeyStream$. Let the key which is generated first be k, and the other one be k'.
   - If $r_j = k$, *outsourcer* accepts $o_j = 0$ as the jth bit of the result.
   - If $r_j = k'$, *outsourcer* accepts $o_j = 1$ as the jth bit of the result.
   - If $r_j \notin \{k, k'\}$, *outsourcer* concludes that *evaluator* tried to cheat, and rejects the received result r. The protocol terminates.

   Let o be the bit string whose j^{th} bit is o_j. If $r_j \in \{k, k'\}$ for all j, then *outsourcer* accepts o as the verified result of the computation.
6. If $l > 0$ (i.e. if there is a layer to peel), *outsourcer* sends the unused garbled inputs g_i' to *evaluator*.
7. **Onion peeling:** In order to prepare for the next computation, *evaluator* peels the outermost layer using g_i' (Section 3.3).
8. Both *outsourcer* and *evaluator* decrement l by one.

5　Proof of Security

This section discusses the security of the protocol with respect to the verifiability property. We follow the formalization of verifiable computation presented in [7]. The security of the protocol is expressed in Theorem 2. First, we note the differences between the "garbled" circuits in the garbled onion construction and Yao's garbled circuits, and define the former based on the differences.

Definition 1. *An onion-garbled circuit (OGC) is a construction built in the same way as a garbled circuit, with the following exceptions:*

- **Fact 1:** *ETT rows are not permuted for any of the gates.*
- **Fact 2:** *Let $k_{out,j}^{b_j}$ be the keys associated with the output wires of the circuit, where $j \in \{0, \ldots, n-1\}$, n is the bit-length of the output, and $b_j \in \{0, 1\}$ is the value assigned to wire j during the in-the-clear evaluation. $k_{out,j}^{b_j}$ are assigned from a keystream $OutKeyStream$ generated by a stream cipher $\mathcal{SC}$ (instead of being randomly assigned).*
- **Fact 3:** *Rest of the keys are not necessarily randomly assigned (but assigned from the ETT rows of another OGC, as described in Sect. 3.1).*

The following lemma is intuitively clear, so it is stated without a proof.

Lemma 1. *Yao's GC construction is still correct when all ETT row permutations are the identity permutation, and when the keys are chosen arbitrarily (rather than randomly).*

Theorem 1. *An OGC provides one-time secure verifiable computation.*

Proof. (sketch) We argue the one-time secure verifiable property of an OGC, based on that of a GC. Gennaro et al. [6, Theorem 3] show that Yao's garbled circuit scheme is a one-time secure verifiable computation scheme.[8] Their proof depends only on the correctness of Yao's garbled circuit construction, and not on its privacy. By Lemma 1, an OGC is also correct. The proof for one-time secure verifiable property of Yao's GC construction can be informally expressed as follows: in order to cheat successfully, the evaluator must either correctly guess a key which was not revealed during evaluation, or break the encryption scheme used for encrypting the circuit. It is the possibility of guessing the keys that requires our attention, because selection of keys differ between a GC and an OGC. Following a computation, the evaluator learns that one of the two keys associated with output wire j is $k_{out,j}^{b_j}$. If the stream cipher SC used for generating $OutKeyStream$ is secure, the revealed keys do not give an adversarial evaluator non-negligible advantage for guessing $k_{out,j}^{1-b_j}$. Therefore the one-time secure verifiable property of an OGC can be argued along the same lines as for a GC, except instead of relying on the fact that keys are chosen randomly, one has to consider the security of SC, and rely on the resulting pseudorandomness of $OutKeyStream$. Intuitively, the enabling property behind the verifiability provided by GCs is that the evaluator is able to open at most one row from each gate, given inputs for a single computation, and this property holds for both GCs and OGCs despite their differences (Facts 1–3).

Theorem 2. *The Protocol for Verifiable Outsourcing using Garbled Onions (Sect. 4) provides up to N verifiable computations, if the garbled onion constructed in the preprocessing phase has N layers.*

Proof. (sketch) First, we observe that a new OGC is constructed for each of the N layers. By Theorem 1, each OGC provides one-time secure verifiable computation. However, the OGCs are constructed in an interdependent fashion, so it is necessary to show that previous computations do not compromise the verifiability of later computations. Consider the $(N-l)^{th}$ computation which uses layer l of the garbled onion. In order to cheat successfully, the evaluator must correctly guess a key which was not revealed during evaluation. But different from the case in Theorem 1, the evaluator is in possession of all the keys in $OutKeyStream$ which are associated with layers $l_i > l$, in addition to the keys revealed during the current computation $(k_{out,j}^{b_j})$. If the stream cipher used for generating $OutKeyStream$ is secure, knowledge of these keys do not give an adversarial

---

[8] This justifies the previously mentioned *inherent verifiability* claim regarding secure 2-party computations using GCs.

evaluator non-negligible advantage for guessing $k_{out,j}^{1-b_j}$. Finally, we note that the keys $k_{out,j}^{1-b_j}$ for layer l are revealed to the evaluator (Online Phase, Step 6) only after the verification for layer l is completed (Online Phase, Step 5).

6 Implementation

This section introduces FairEnough [4], a proof-of-concept implementation of the onion garbling technique and the protocol for verifiable outsourcing described in Sect. 4. Each of the three parties involved in the protocol are implemented in their own classes (`Outsourcer`, `Evaluator`, `Constructor`), and they communicate via TCP sockets to run the protocol. The implementation is based on Fairplay [14], which dates back to 2004. Several CG optimizations (e.g. free-XOR [13], GRR2 [17], FleXOR [12], half gates [20]) have been developed since that time, and these optimizations are not included in Fairplay.[9] As mentioned in Sect. 3.1, onion garbling takes a different approach compared to these optimizations, and Fairplay was a suitable starting point for our implementation due to being uncluttered with incompatible optimizations. The main functionality kept from the original Fairplay project is the generation of circuit objects from SFDL programs via the SFDL compiler, circuit optimizer, and SHDL parser. SFDL programs describe a 2-party computation, where both parties (referred to as Alice and Bob in Fairplay) may have inputs and outputs. In case of outsourcing, we assume that only the outsourcing party has inputs and outputs. The outsourced computation is described as an SFDL program with only `BobInput` and `BobOutput`, which represent the outsourcer's inputs and the outputs, respectively.

7 Conclusion

This work tackled an efficiency issue related to the use of garbled circuits for verifiable computations, which arise from the single-use nature of a garbled circuit. The onion garbling technique was introduced, which leverage the freedom in the assignment of keys during the construction of a garbled circuit, in order to encode many garbled circuits into a single one. A protocol for verifiable computations, which utilize the onion garbling technique, was proposed. The protocol achieves N-reusability in the sense that the memory and communication cost of N verifiable computations is significantly less compared to the trivial solution, which involves the construction and transfer of N distinct garbled circuits. But most importantly, the costs incurred on the outsourcing party is sufficiently small to allow verifiable outsourcing by a resource-constrained device on a constrained network.

---

[9] For a more recent, optimized framework for circuit garbling, see for example [9].

8   Future Work

This work addressed a major obstacle to practical verifiable outsourcing using GCs, namely the single-use nature of the constructed GCs. Another major obstacle to practical verifiable outsourcing using GCs is the size and runtime inflation due to the conversion to Boolean circuit. Running both branches for each branching, and running each loop the maximum number of times it can be run give the resulting circuit its obliviousness property. Obliviousness is essential when privacy is desired, but not when the only security goal is verifiability. In the proposed protocol, the evaluator is provided with the knowledge of the inputs and the computation, and is able to perform the in-the-clear computation. In this case, it would be a good trade-off to let go off the obliviousness property, if in turn the size and runtime inflation could be eliminated. This suggests moving away from the circuit model of computation, but of course one would want to keep the verifiability which comes with the garbled circuit evaluations. Investigation of the applicability of onion garbling beyond the circuit model of computation is left as future work.

The proof-of-concept implementation introduced in Sect. 6 was useful in writing parts of this work, as following working source code provides some degree of reassurance against possible errors and omissions during the textual description of the ideas. We believe that the codebase could prove to be a useful resource for the motivated reader as well, for clarifying ambiguities and filling in gaps, caused by weaknesses in our writing. We note however that, the implementation was not meant to assess feasibility, and deployment on an actual resource-constrained device is left as future work.

Acknowledgements. This work is supported in part by Tekes under the project Wireless for Verticals (WIVE). WIVE is a part of 5G Test Network Finland (5GTNF). We thank Ethiopia Nigussie for encouraging us to think about applications of secure multiparty computation in the context of the Internet of Things and Edge Computing. Finally, the author would like to thank the anonymous reviewers for their valuable comments.

References

1. Applebaum, B., Ishai, Y., Kushilevitz, E.: From secrecy to soundness: efficient verification via secure computation. In: Abramsky, S., Gavoille, C., Kirchner, C., Meyer auf der Heide, F., Spirakis, P.G. (eds.) ICALP 2010. LNCS, vol. 6198, pp. 152–163. Springer, Heidelberg (2010). https://doi.org/10.1007/978-3-642-14165-2_14
2. Beaver, D., Micali, S., Rogaway, P.: The round complexity of secure protocols. In: Proceedings of the Twenty-Second Annual ACM Symposium on Theory of Computing, STOC 1990, pp. 503–513. ACM, New York (1990). https://doi.org/10.1145/100216.100287
3. Bellare, M., Hoang, V.T., Rogaway, P.: Foundations of garbled circuits. In: Proceedings of the 2012 ACM Conference on Computer and Communications Security, CCS 2012, pp. 784–796. ACM, New York (2012). https://doi.org/10.1145/2382196.2382279

4. Dönmez, T.C.M.: Fairenough, July 2018. https://gitlab.utu.fi/tcmdon/Fairenough
5. Dworkin, M.: Recommendation for block cipher modes of operation. Methods and techniques. Technical report, National Institute of Standards and Technology, Gaithersburg, MD. Computer Security Division, December 2001. http://www.dtic.mil/docs/citations/ADA400014
6. Gennaro, R., Gentry, C., Parno, B.: Non-interactive verifiable computing: outsourcing computation to untrusted workers. Cryptology ePrint Archive, Report 2009/547 (2009). https://eprint.iacr.org/2009/547
7. Gennaro, R., Gentry, C., Parno, B.: Non-interactive verifiable computing: outsourcing computation to untrusted workers. In: Rabin, T. (ed.) CRYPTO 2010. LNCS, vol. 6223, pp. 465–482. Springer, Heidelberg (2010). https://doi.org/10.1007/978-3-642-14623-7_25
8. Goldwasser, S., Kalai, Y., Popa, R.A., Vaikuntanathan, V., Zeldovich, N.: Reusable garbled circuits and succinct functional encryption. In: Proceedings of the Forty-Fifth Annual ACM Symposium on Theory of Computing, STOC 2013, pp. 555–564. ACM, New York (2013). https://doi.org/10.1145/2488608.2488678
9. Huang, Y., Shen, C., Evans, D., Katz, J., Shelat, A.: Efficient secure computation with garbled circuits. In: Jajodia, S., Mazumdar, C. (eds.) ICISS 2011. LNCS, vol. 7093, pp. 28–48. Springer, Heidelberg (2011). https://doi.org/10.1007/978-3-642-25560-1_2
10. Ishai, Y., Wee, H.: Partial garbling schemes and their applications. In: Esparza, J., Fraigniaud, P., Husfeldt, T., Koutsoupias, E. (eds.) ICALP 2014. LNCS, vol. 8572, pp. 650–662. Springer, Heidelberg (2014). https://doi.org/10.1007/978-3-662-43948-7_54
11. Keranen, A., Ersue, M., Bormann, C.: Terminology for constrained-node networks. RFC 7228, RFC Editor, May 2014. https://doi.org/10.17487/RFC7228, http://www.rfc-editor.org/info/rfc7228
12. Kolesnikov, V., Mohassel, P., Rosulek, M.: FleXOR: flexible garbling for XOR gates that beats free-XOR. In: Garay, J.A., Gennaro, R. (eds.) CRYPTO 2014. LNCS, vol. 8617, pp. 440–457. Springer, Heidelberg (2014). https://doi.org/10.1007/978-3-662-44381-1_25
13. Kolesnikov, V., Schneider, T.: Improved garbled circuit: free XOR gates and applications. In: Aceto, L., Damgård, I., Goldberg, L.A., Halldórsson, M.M., Ingólfsdóttir, A., Walukiewicz, I. (eds.) ICALP 2008. LNCS, vol. 5126, pp. 486–498. Springer, Heidelberg (2008). https://doi.org/10.1007/978-3-540-70583-3_40
14. Malkhi, D., Nisan, N., Pinkas, B., Sella, Y.: Fairplay–a secure two-party computation system. In: Proceedings of the 13th Conference on USENIX Security Symposium, SSYM 2004, vol. 13, p. 20. USENIX Association, Berkeley (2004). http://dl.acm.org/citation.cfm?id=1251375.1251395
15. Naor, M., Pinkas, B., Sumner, R.: Privacy preserving auctions and mechanism design. In: Proceedings of the 1st ACM Conference on Electronic Commerce, EC 1999, pp. 129–139. ACM, New York (1999). https://doi.org/10.1145/336992.337028
16. Parno, B., Howell, J., Gentry, C., Raykova, M.: Pinocchio: nearly practical verifiable computation. In: 2013 IEEE Symposium on Security and Privacy, pp. 238–252, May 2013. https://doi.org/10.1109/SP.2013.47
17. Pinkas, B., Schneider, T., Smart, N.P., Williams, S.C.: Secure two-party computation is practical. In: Matsui, M. (ed.) ASIACRYPT 2009. LNCS, vol. 5912, pp. 250–267. Springer, Heidelberg (2009). https://doi.org/10.1007/978-3-642-10366-7_15

18. Yao, A.C.: Protocols for secure computations. In: 23rd Annual Symposium on Foundations of Computer Science (SFCS 1982), pp. 160–164, November 1982. https://doi.org/10.1109/SFCS.1982.38
19. Yao, A.C.C.: How to generate and exchange secrets. In: 27th Annual Symposium on Foundations of Computer Science (SFCS 1986), pp. 162–167, October 1986. https://doi.org/10.1109/SFCS.1986.25
20. Zahur, S., Rosulek, M., Evans, D.: Two halves make a whole. In: Oswald, E., Fischlin, M. (eds.) EUROCRYPT 2015. LNCS, vol. 9057, pp. 220–250. Springer, Heidelberg (2015). https://doi.org/10.1007/978-3-662-46803-6_8

Author Index

Printed in the United States
By Bookmasters